CRYSTAL BROADCASTING

USING CRYSTALS TO REMOVE BLOCKS & BARRIERS

****

Anne Brewer

INTERLINK

Crystal Broadcasting
Using Crystals To Remove Blocks & Barriers
by Anne Brewer

InterLink Publishing, Inc.
5252 W. 67th Street
Prairie Village, KS 66208

LCCN: 2001097047
ISBN: 0-9710563-3-1

Cover design and production by
Arthur Durkee, Holistic Marketing Cooperative

Printed in the U.S.A.

Readers interested in obtaining further information on the subject matter of this book are invited to correspond with:

InterLink Publishing, Inc.
5252 W. 67th Street
Prairie Village, KS 66208
913-722-5498
info@annebrewer.com
For more InterLink books, please visit our website:
www.annebrewer.com

TABLE OF CONTENTS

≈≈≈≈≈≈≈≈≈≈≈≈≈≈≈≈≈

Chapter 4 (continued)
Modeling Abilities of Popular Crystals

Chapter 5
Energy States and Corresponding Crystals

Chapter 6
Using a Pendulum to Dowse for the Optimal Crystal

Chapter 7
Dowsing for the Optimal Crystal

≈≈≈≈≈≈≈≈≈≈≈≈≈≈≈≈

Chapter 7 (continued)
Dowsing for the Optimal Crystal

Chapter 8
Balancing Chakras with Crystal Broadcasting

Appendix

≈≈≈≈≈≈≈≈≈≈≈≈≈≈≈≈≈

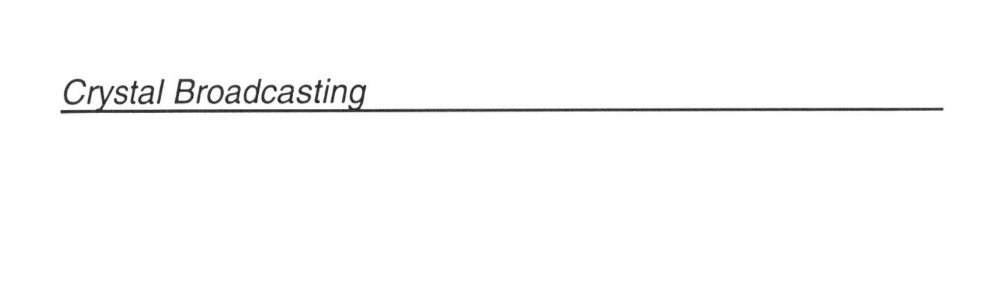

≈≈≈≈≈≈≈≈≈≈≈≈≈≈≈≈

INTRODUCTION

"Within every human being, there are gods and goddesses in embryo with only one desire. They want to be born."
Deepak Chopra

Crystal Broadcasting is a "metaphysical cookbook." It provides simple recipes for removing undesirable behaviors, enabling us to release the god or goddess embryo that resides inside us. We may have a vision of our potential perfection, but it gets lost among the daily pressures that stimulate "negative" rather than "positive" responses. As the pace of life quickens, the mounting strain takes its toll, exacerbating negative reactions that might be easier to control during calmer moments. Broadcasting with crystals offers an extremely simple and effective healing modality for removing tiresome negative behaviors. Good habits can replace bad habits -- New Year's resolutions can become a reality!

Everyone has behaviors they want to eliminate. Some of these behaviors are annoying while others are life-threatening. For example, you might be quite aware of a habit of impatience. You may experience it multiple times and always regret losing your cool or making a quick but inaccurate assumption. Despite your dislike of your behavior and your resolution to change it, impatience surfaces again and again. Other types of undesirable behaviors are more insidious and more difficult to hide from others or control. These are categorized as addictions or obsessions. Drinking alcohol or taking drugs are typical of the types of persistent addictive behaviors that affect health, relationships, financial security, and perhaps even careers. Obsessions are equally harmful because they cause us to fixate over someone or something, eradicating any possibility of balance or harmony in life.

≈≈≈≈≈≈≈≈≈≈≈≈≈≈≈≈

Whether annoying or life-threatening, most people want to alter their negative behaviors. Yet, despite the desire to improve, we tend to perpetuate these behaviors. We know the behavior, and we do not want it. Yet, it continues to persist, sometimes after years of therapy. In fact, we might become so discouraged by persistent negative habits that we learn to adapt to them. It's the old motto – "If you can't beat 'em, join 'em." Or, we may even ignore them, determining that we will solve the problem by surrounding ourselves with people who either have high tolerance levels or mirror our same behavior. Why do we seem to get stuck with unwanted behaviors, despite our desire to change? The answer lies in the way we are structured.

Human beings consist of more energy than matter. In fact, we are comprised of 99.9% empty space and .1% molecular structure. The quantum physicists have proven that we are primarily constructed of energy rather than matter. In alternative therapies, the energy is called the "aura" or "subtle bodies." In science, the energy is called the electromagnetic field. If we consist mostly of an energy field, we have the capacity to alter our behaviors by changing our energy vibration. Since we are composed mainly of empty space, it is easy to repattern our energy blueprint. We just need to know how to do it. Our molecules respond very quickly to vibrations like light, sound, and color by altering patterns. Repatterning is just like asking an architect to renovate a house, altering the original blueprint to create a new living space. In *Crystal Broadcasting*, you will learn how to use the energy vibration of crystals to repattern yourself. Crystals are just like positive intentions that have been frozen. They hold a specific energy pattern that can be broadcasted for you until you, yourself, are able to fully embrace the upgraded behavior.

≈≈≈≈≈≈≈≈≈≈≈≈≈≈≈≈

Crystal Broadcasting is based on the assumption that we pick up energetic patterns that may serve us at one point in our life but eventually outgrow their usefulness. Or, they may have never really served us but seemed like the best idea at the time. In his book *Surfers of the Zuvuya*, José Argüelles describes the human energy field as a wave form. Our wave form picks up static cling as we move through our life experiences. Static might come in the form of negative messages experienced as a child, e.g., "you're a mess", "you're acting like an idiot", "you can't do anything right", that result in compensatory behaviors in adulthood that do not get us what we really want. Or static might occur when we learn safe behaviors, e.g., complying with authority figures like teachers or bosses, and these ingrained behavioral responses might conflict with our desire to be something else, perhaps a forward-thinker and a creative problem-solver.

Most people are trained to employ mind over matter to facilitate change. We try to alter our physical situation rather than changing our energy blueprint and allowing physical change to follow suit. The architect creates the plan before, not after, renovating the house! As an extreme example, I knew someone who was very obese so he was always trying new diets. After years of unsuccessful dieting (mind over matter), he had part of his stomach "stapled" to limit his food intake, and he dropped over one hundred pounds. But, when the doctor removed the staples, my friend began eating again. He had not changed his energy blueprint that relied on food for emotional fulfillment. It might have been more productive for him to focus on the emotional discord that promoted his excessive eating. Overeating could have been resolved by first repatterning unwanted energy vibrations in order to create new habits.

≈≈≈≈≈≈≈≈≈≈≈≈≈≈≈≈≈

Crystal Broadcasting combines the use of crystals, affirmations, and sacred geometry to create a powerful healing process. The crystals broadcast the intended desire, just like crystals are used in radio broadcasting because of their excellent transmitting capabilities. The affirmations identify the "New Year's" resolution that requires broadcasting. The sacred geometry, called a Universal Symbol, models the affirmations so the universe can interpret and support them. The Universal Symbol holds the creation codes of the universe, as explained in books on sacred geometry. Since we are electromagnetic fields of energy, we can broadcast any frequency with which we resonate. Based on the law of attraction, our dominant frequencies are matched with corresponding vibrations. That is why, for example, "the rich get richer and the poor get poorer" or "birds of a feather flock together". *Crystal Broadcasting* explains the energy make-up of the human body, the law of attraction, and the crystal broadcasting process that overrides unwanted negative vibrations in order to help us get what we want.

As a metaphysical coach and healer, I have helped many people alter their toxic behavior patterns by repatterning the root cause of their disorders. My background as a vice president of marketing in the telecommunications field and my role as president of my own marketing consulting firm enable me to blend my intuitive information with a disciplined and grounded approach that makes sense to people. In my healing practice, I am continually encountering people who are anxious to do their own clearing work. However, they do not always have the tools to work on their own issues. *Crystal Broadcasting* is my effort to share some tools so that you can take your healing process into your own hands.

≈≈≈≈≈≈≈≈≈≈≈≈≈≈≈≈

No one wants to be less than they can be. When people are provided with an effective healing tool, the majority wholeheartedly embrace that tool if it clears unwanted behaviors. People desire freedom from their bad habits. They enjoy saving the time and expense spent on a cadre of healing practitioners that might not always reach the root of the problem. They relish the self-empowerment that occurs when able to heal themselves. *Crystal Broadcasting* provides recipes that the average, non-psychic person can follow, recipes that create savory results.

Peace,
Anne Brewer

≈≈≈≈≈≈≈≈≈≈≈≈≈≈≈≈

CHAPTER 1

DISCOVERING HOW TO BROADCAST WITH CRYSTALS

Metaphysics versus Business

My life is very diverse because I have two distinctly different orientation and skill sets. On the one hand, I am a metaphysical author, teacher, and healer. I write books about new age topics, and I conduct seminars and private sessions on the same material. On the other hand, I am a business person. I was employed in corporate America for almost two decades which culminated in a vice-president position in the field of telecommunications. Following a successful corporate career, I developed my own marketing consulting business that I have enjoyed managing since 1992. Needless to say, I bridge two worlds. In my metaphysical work, I tend to rely on highly intuitive right brain information that I receive from the etheric realm via my. In business, I use my analytical left brain faculties in conjunction with data derived through my tactical senses.

My husband, David, admires my ability to represent both worlds. He feels my intuitive side has increased my propensity for business success, and my analytical side has infused my healing work with practicality. As a Doctor of Chiropractic, a Clinical Nutritionist, and a teacher of the ancient Polynesian Huna philosophy, David is naturally inclined to enjoy my diversity since he, too, integrates right and left-brain talents. In fact, he is the one who affectionately accuses me of writing "metaphysical cookbooks." He sees how my intuitive side receives the telepathic transmissions and my mental side develops detailed instructions on how to achieve the intended state.

Personally, I often feel like I am in the middle of an identity crisis due to my right-brain/left-brain careers.

≈≈≈≈≈≈≈≈≈≈≈≈≈≈≈≈≈

Although I am currently in my late forties, I still don't know what I want to be when I grow up. When I attempt to leave the business world to immerse myself in metaphysical teaching and healing, I miss the straightforward routines, well-defined goals and objectives, and orientation toward the future that is characterized by business. Then, when I increase my marketing consulting work, I miss the creative thought processes that lead to new insights in my metaphysical work and the personal connections with my clients. Am I a metaphysical healer or a business consultant? Is there a place in this world for a logical psychic?

Perhaps, the answer is "yes." Since my left-brain orientation creates objectivity and order, I write how-to manuals. Many of my healing modalities are structured like recipes. You mix together one white candle, five cleansing breaths, and two affirmations and meditate for fifteen minutes until done. During my corporate business years, I wrote many strategic marketing documents such as business plans, sales force procedures, and market research reports. I was accustomed to creating a plan, communicating it to the work team, and implementing it. I am more comfortable knowing where I am going and how well I am doing. At this point in my spiritual development, I know I should have developed a sense of living in the "now" and an innate feeling of Divine order. However, my training in business planning persists, and I like to know where I stand. My healing work is characterized by checkpoints that enable people to evaluate their progress.

Broadcasting with Crystals

If you are the type of person who desires to expand your spirituality, but you feel more comfortable when you can integrate logic and reason with creativity and intuition, then you will enjoy this book. *Crystal Broadcasting* is a "how-to" book. You can conduct crystal healing by spending a couple of hours perusing the book and becoming comfortable with how to use it. You do not need to take a 3-day course to learn a complex process. You do not need to complete an in-depth study on the properties of the various crystals. You do not need to be telepathic to receive psychic information.

The information on broadcasting with crystals was gifted to me by "Spirit." I asked Spirit to assist me in developing a simple process that enables people to break free from limitations by clearing subconscious blocks. According to Gunther Bernard, "We choose to forget who we are and then forget we've forgotten." We often "forget" because it is too painful to remember. I recently worked with a woman who could not hold an adjustment for more than a few days following a visit to her chiropractor. After her last appointment, she went next door to the supermarket to food shop and fell against a cart, injuring herself and undoing what had just been done. These are the types of clues that the subconscious provides if we choose to pay attention to them. When we examined her motivations, we determined she was subconsciously creating discomfort in her body because this was her way of receiving attention as a child. Her parents led busy lives and tended to ignore her. However, they could not ignore her when she was sick, staying home from work to administer to her. As an adult, she was able to receive attention from her doctor, albeit an expensive method of eliciting attention. Her core issue was the lack of attention from her parents, which she chose to forget because it was too painful to think they might not love her. By surfacing the core issue, we had something that we could address and heal.

Paying attention to continued negative outcomes is the first step toward healing. It is our subconscious crying for help. However, our subconscious has grown accustomed to habits that achieve results, even if those results aren't satisfactory, i.e., attention via pain instead of love. We need to model the new behavior that we truly desire until our subconscious can catch up with us. How do we project the new attitudes until the behaviors follow suit? It is unfeasible to repeat affirmations hundreds of times per day. In fact, it is unrealistic to expect people to even remember to affirm for the new behavior. It became obvious to me that I needed to develop a method to "hold" the desired state until the new behavior became entrenched.

I eventually reached a solution to this dilemma One of my favorite methods of receiving information from Spirit is to float in my swimming pool. I was in my pool one day, ruminating over the need to develop a method to hold positive energy until unwanted behaviors had changed, and I received the crystal broadcasting information from Spirit. When I purchased my house, I did not want a pool but I loved the house and overcame my resistance toward the pool. Eventually, it became my "think tank" as I discovered I could lie on a raft and descend into an alpha state. My conscious self would retreat so I could hear information from Spirit. I received much information on healing modalities, topics for books, and seminar contents. As always, there is a reason and purpose for everything!

While floating in the pool during the summer of 1998, my Spirit guides began describing how we can use the broadcasting nature of crystals to alter negative behavior patterns. Please note that when I refer to crystals, I am using that word to encompass minerals and gemstones. The process that Spirit communicated was simple. Essentially, we could define the behavior that was no longer desirable. Then, we could identify the converse of that behavior, or the positive intention that was desired. The desired state was to be written on a piece of paper, called a Resolution Sheet. A Universal Symbol needed to be developed to slide underneath the piece of paper that contained the desired state. Spirit assured me it would provide the means of developing the Universal Symbol. The Universal Symbol would molecularly represent every creation code in the universe so the desired intention could be interpreted, i.e., whatever was written on the Resolution Sheet was identifiable in the vibrational language of the universe. Finally, a crystal that corresponded to the desired energy was to be placed on top of the words describing the intended state. The crystal would continuously broadcast the identified vibration. According to the law of attraction, the vibration would attract and coalesce with matching vibrations, creating a great deal of momentum around the desired state, thereby overriding the undesirable state.

I was overjoyed to receive this information. It was relatively simple, and anyone can do it. Crystals were widely available and, even if someone did not have a rock shop in their vicinity, they could access the Internet for numerous rock and mineral websites or purchase *Lapidary Journal* and contact the rock shops that advertised by telephone. In fact, I ultimately discovered that a clear quartz crystal could be used for "all-purpose," albeit slower, clearings since clear quartz did not hold a specific program like the other crystals did. I envisioned that I could give people an explanation of how the process worked, identify the crystal they needed to use, give them a copy of the Universal Symbol, and they could procure their crystal and facilitate their own healing.

Based on my knowledge of the ancient Polynesian Huna doctrine, I also liked the tangible aspect of the broadcasting process. The Kahunas believed the soul is comprised of three parts: the low, middle, and high self. In modern terms, we call these parts the subconscious, conscious, and superconscious. The subconscious is the seat of our emotions and memory. Because it has instinctual behavior, the subconscious is often illogical in its processing of life's events. In

≈≈≈≈≈≈≈≈≈≈≈≈≈≈≈≈

fact, most of the time, healing simply requires the illogical agenda that has become entrenched in the subconscious to be aligned with the logical needs of the conscious. The Kahunas employed ritual as a means of impressing the low self with something real and tangible to release memory programs that no longer served it.

For example, a person may hold a pattern of unworthiness after being raised by hyper-critical parents. The memories held by the subconscious are illogical since a toddler cannot assess his or her parent's shortcomings and determine the criticism is unfounded. When that child becomes an adult, the lack of worthiness may appear in an inability to manifest what he or she desires. The conscious adult may want something, but the subconscious part of the soul feels unworthy to receive it. The conscious is frustrated by opportunities that have been blocked, not realizing that the subconscious has caused the lack of success by feeling unworthy. By performing a real and tangible exercise, perhaps having the adult participate in an act of service that benefits the community while relating these acts of service to worthiness, the subconscious releases the old programming.

The Catholic ritual of confession is a good example of how the real and tangible aspect of ritual works to reprogram the subconscious self. When the subconscious feels guilty, it does not cooperate with our desires at a conscious level. By entering a small, dark confessional and sharing "secrets" with a priestly adviser who has the ear of God, the subconscious is impressed by the seriousness of the event. Then, the priest blesses the person and removes the sins, much to the relief of the emotion-laden subconscious. Sometimes, the priest requires additional homework in the form of prayers or acts of service that further impress the subconscious that all guilt has been resolved. Thus, the conscious self is freed from subconscious restrictions because there is no guilt or shame.

When you ask your subconscious to write down the new condition you wish to embrace, it performs a real and tangible task. Then, when you place the Universal Symbol under the Resolution Sheet and the crystal on top, you are enacting a ritual that is also impressive to the subconscious. Essentially, you have begun the repatterning process before the crystal starts broadcasting!

I spent several years researching the various crystals and their properties. I also tested the process on myself, my friends, and my clients. It really works! The Resolution Sheet outlines the issues that need to be broadcast. The crystal models the identified issues. And, the Universal Symbol interprets the issues so they can be understood. The information is broadcast twenty-four hours a day, seven days a week, so you do not need to continually hold your resolutions in the forefront of your mind. The entire process and how it works will be explained in the next chapter.

Testing the Process

I tend to use more masculine than feminine energy when interacting with people, perhaps because of my corporate management training. Based on some urogenital difficulties I was experiencing, I developed an interest in increasing my feminine energy. I felt I could repattern the root cause of my physical problems by increasing my female energy.

I was raised in the South in the 1950's, and young girls were cultivated to be help-mates to their future husbands. I was expected to marry, work prior to having children but not have a "career," stop working after having children, and be a stay-at-home mom until the children left for college. For some reason,

≈≈≈≈≈≈≈≈≈≈≈≈≈≈≈≈

this pre-determined path for females was not appealing to me. I rejected the assumption that I had to be a help-mate rather than a wage-earner. I wanted to be recognized as a career person as well as a wife and mother. These were novel ideas in the 1950's when most girls played house and shared dreams of marrying and raising a family.

As a teenager, I was rebellious as I tried to establish a career-oriented identity. I purposely dropped my Southern accent and substituted jeans for dresses since my blond hair and Southern drawl were interfering with my ability to be taken "seriously." I posed as an intellectual, raising and debating ecological, political, and social issues. I insisted I would never marry or have children since I would be busy with my career. My family began referring to me as "difficult" as they were unsure of how to handle my attitude.

Until recently, I did not realize what I lost by discarding my feminine self. My masculine orientation persisted throughout my young adult years. I rigorously pursued a career rather than focusing on marriage and family. I did not marry until I was thirty, which is common now but was not then. I was determined to continue pursuing my corporate career despite the birth of my child. I worked until the day I delivered my son, Andrew, and I returned to work exactly six weeks later at the end of the designated maternity leave. I had become more masculine than feminine. I was characterized as assertive and demanding rather than soft and yielding. As I eventually realized, we benefit most by an even balance of masculine and feminine traits. Gender style flexibility is important for a balanced life, regardless of our physical gender.

As a first step toward embracing my feminine, I followed some gender balance instructions that Spirit provided. This resulted in a better balance between my masculine and feminine sides, and it enabled me to project a softer, more appropriate demeanor when conducting healing work with my clients. However, I was still carrying emotional patterns that conflicted with my feminine side. My husband attempted to discuss my imbalance, but I became angry because I felt he was critical. He stopped raising this delicate topic. He knew I would not be receptive to his observations until I was ready to address the situation.

I began to develop physical symptoms in my female system that I could no longer ignore. I had experienced some questionable pap smears prior to meeting my husband. Although I eventually cleared the emotional blockage and began receiving normal pap smears, other female-related symptoms began to surface. I was plagued with urinary tract infections. My subconscious (which is responsible for automatic body functions like breathing, pulse rate, blinking) was not ignoring my remaining feminine-based issues like I was! It chose to rebel whenever my feminine side was required to surface. It felt unsafe when the soft side of me emerged, equating it to my earlier conclusion that softness would get trampled in a male-oriented world.

After I obtained the information from Spirit on broadcasting via crystals, I decided to test it by addressing my persistent, annoying infections. At the time, I still did not accept the association between my female issues and infections, but I was weary of the cranberry juice and oregano oil that was necessary to kill the infection. I determined which crystal I needed to use, a process I will describe later. I placed the crystal, which happened to be citrine, on top of the sheet of paper specifying the feminine energy I desired, and I inserted the Universal Symbol underneath the Resolution Sheet. I left it undisturbed on my closet shelf.

≈≈≈≈≈≈≈≈≈≈≈≈≈≈≈≈

Within two weeks, I felt very motivated to contact a spiritual counselor that resides in Sedona. I had met her during a past trip to the area and had worked with her several times by telephone. I scheduled an appointment, unsure what we would discuss but knowing it was important to speak with her. During the appointment, I told her I desired a read-out of my present spiritual condition. She told me how males represented electrical energy while females represented magnetic energy, and she did not find sufficient magnetic energy around me. In fact, she said we were evolving into an androgynous society, and the lack of female energy was a planetary concern for our evolution. I was surprised, realizing that the crystal had already drawn into my life the information I needed to hear to assist in reconciling my situation. Apparently, I had achieved gender balance in terms of style flexibility. However, I had not yet achieved balance in the electric and magnetic frequencies that surrounded my body. While the citrine crystal was broadcasting and modeling my desire for feminine energy, it had also drawn someone to me who could augment the process by reinforcing the importance of embracing my female magnetic energy.

Later, when my husband listened to the tape of my counseling session, he noted the similarity to his information. As most married couples can attest, somehow the same advice sounds different when receiving it from someone else! Perhaps, I needed to hear an interpretation from a fellow female to be receptive. Or, maybe I felt less vulnerable being told I was not perfect by someone other than my husband.

The session with the counselor caused me to wholeheartedly embrace the notion of expanding my feminine side. I would not disappear into the woodwork and become invisible by allowing my feminine or soft side to show. I would not be less successful as a business person by showing my feminine attributes. These were notions I had adopted as a child and my subconscious continued to hold onto them. Now I could feel safe releasing these notions that no longer served me. In fact, the counselor said it would be easier to conduct business with more feminine energy since the female represented "creation" energy while the male represented "producing" energy. If I increased my feminine energy, I would conduct my work by "flowing" rather than by "doing" which would enable the work to feel effortless rather than battling resistance to get things done.

The counselor provided some suggestions on how I could increase my level of magnetic energy. Based on this timely information, I was able to simultaneously conduct her recommended healing modalities while my crystal was holding the enhanced feminine energy I desired. I was doubly productive. I was impressed by how quickly the crystal had attracted some of the information I needed in order to complete my healing. The broadcasting structure had beckoned someone to assist me. This was my first understanding about the broadcasting process in terms of how it acted as a beacon to attract propitious information or experiences. I had to adjust my perception of how the healing would occur, having assumed the crystal would restructure my energy rather than acting as a guiding light to illuminate my healing options in addition to holding the behavior pattern I wished to emulate.

Continuing the Test

The following month, I received a call from a Kansas City couple who had moved to Salt Lake City. I was friends with them during their residency in town, and I missed them. They were returning to Kansas City for the sale of their home, and they wanted to meet me for dinner. As we caught up on life's events over our meal, my friend mentioned a healing she experienced with a gifted energy worker who lived in California. As she shared the work from her session, I noted how strongly my heart resonated with her experience. I knew I was supposed to call her healer. I asked for the telephone number, but, since my friends had just moved, she could not recall where she had put the information. Knowing that the universe always works in perfect timing, I waited an additional month for the contact information. In the meanwhile, my crystal continued to clear on my behalf since information from Spirit instructed me to leave the crystal in place.

I finally received the contact information, and I scheduled an appointment with the energy worker. During my session, the healer read my energy field. She said I had a blockage that did not allow my sexual energy to easily connect with my heart. She could see that I was more comfortable living "outside" my body, communing with Spirit rather than embracing the physical experience. This was no surprise since I had spent the last ten years trying to overcome my tendency to reject the physical experience. I had typically been uncomfortable in my body and had tried to "escape" through mental gymnastics and creative fantasies. I misunderstood that we are Spirit having a physical experience. However, I eventually came to realize I had requested a physical body for a reason and was trying to reconcile my dissatisfaction so I could experience soul growth through the physical experience. Could this be another layer that was part of my feminine energy block? Not only had I rejected the feminine, I had also rejected my physical body. Intellectually, I knew I had to embrace my physical experience rather than reject it. Now, the rubber was meeting the road!

The energy worker from California tracked back through my multiple past lifetimes where I had felt a lack of sustenance from the earth. Apparently, I had made a vow to rely only on myself for sustenance since I believed, erroneously, that the earth and its occupants had betrayed me. I had experienced starvation, earthquakes, and abusive relationships that undermined my faith. The lack of trust in my physical surroundings and intimate relationships explained why I had excelled in corporate America. I was driven to succeed in a male-oriented world because I was overly focused on my need for security. The healer said I needed to release the vow of self-reliance since it placed me in a masculine state of being, prompting me to produce and produce to ensure my sustenance. She also helped me remove the blockage between my physically-oriented lower energy centers or chakras and my spiritually-oriented upper chakras so I could better blend the energy at my heart center.

Within two months, the crystal had evoked two healers who could assist me in increasing my feminine energy. Within a month of this second healing session, my guides told me the crystal had completed its broadcasting in regard to the identified issue, and it was time to remove it from the Universal Symbol.

Although the broadcasting system brought healers into my life, it is important to point out that it also simultaneously healed my etheric body. The etheric body is the blueprint for the physical body. If everything is balanced in the etheric body, the physical body follows suit. It is much easier to heal physical conditions by first healing the energy or etheric body, because the physical body duplicates the conditions of its energy blueprint. By specifying an issue, holding the molecular pattern of the issue's resolution via the Universal Symbol, and broadcasting the resolution into the universe, my etheric body held my desired vibration 24 hours a day, 7 days a week. The universe simply matched my new vibration, thereby releasing me from my old pattern. I was free to experience my feminine side!

≈≈≈≈≈≈≈≈≈≈≈≈≈≈≈≈

Stumbling Blocks

As I worked with clients and shared the crystal broadcasting process, I encountered several problems. First, some people did not have immediate sources for crystals since they lived in small communities where there were no rock and mineral shops. Second, I had to identify the crystal to use. Although a quartz crystal has a generic energy that can be applied to any issue, it is not necessarily the most targeted approach. Usually, a specific crystal works faster. Finally, some of the crystals I recommended to clients were unavailable on the retail market despite the fact they were listed in metaphysical crystal books. I needed to address these issues in order for people to utilize this process.

The enclosed written information represents the results. I have divided the information into the following sections:

1. A step-by-step overview of the actual process.
2. An interpretation of the Universal Symbol and how it works.
3. Instructions on dowsing with a pendulum to determine the optimal match of the crystal with the issue, assuming a clear quartz crystal is not being used.
4. An alphabetical list of crystals for dowsing purposes.
5. A list of popular crystals and the conditions they model, for those who do not wish to learn to use a pendulum.
6. A list of desirable conditions and the corresponding crystals needed for modeling, again for those who do not wish to use a pendulum.
7. The seven primary chakra centers and the corresponding crystals needed for balancing those centers.
8. Retail sources for crystals and recommended reference books.

≈≈≈≈≈≈≈≈≈≈≈≈≈≈≈≈

Rest assured, this process is very easy, especially if you already know how to dowse with a pendulum. However, even if you do not use a pendulum, you can easily adopt this talent by reading the enclosed material. This way you are ensured of selecting the optimal crystal energy. Or, you can use the tables that tell you which crystal matches your condition. Like me, you may encounter additional assistance as you clear your issues since the crystal is emitting an energy frequency into the universe to create the conditions that need to occur to reconcile your issues. However, it is equally likely you may not need to do anything but allow the crystal to remain in place for a period of time.

≈≈≈≈≈≈≈≈≈≈≈≈≈≈≈≈

≈≈≈≈≈≈≈≈≈≈≈≈≈≈≈≈

CHAPTER 2

THE BROADCASTING PROCESS

The Need for Specificity

The broadcasting process is very simple. Despite its simplicity, it is also very powerful. The healing is most effective when you take the time to specify the issues for clearing and the corresponding desirable intentions before purchasing crystals and laying them on the Universal Symbol. It is easy to put the physical components in place. However, if the issues are not clearly identified, an inappropriate crystal may be selected.

Naturally, the more that you have already begun your healing process, the more quickly the crystal can shift the remaining residue. If you are aware of an issue that needs resolution and have already undertaken healing to address it, the issue responds quickly to broadcasting. For example, by the time I employed the broadcasting process to address my feminine energy, I had already undergone attunement, acupuncture, and repatterning for some of the physical problems I was experiencing. Obviously, my problems were caused by the negativity I held toward my feminine energy. Any healing work I experienced began to peel away the layers that surrounded my issues. Essentially, I had already transmuted some of the negative energy I held. By the time I implemented broadcasting, the remaining clearing was completed in a matter of months since I had already experienced preliminary healing.

The Role of the Subconscious

Often, clients will tell me they no longer need to clear a particular issue I have identified because they "used to" have that problem, but they have already addressed it. When I check with Spirit to determine if their subconscious resonates with a resolution of their situation, they are usually surprised when the answer is “no”. Most of us believe we have resolved negative patterns when we consciously become aware of issues and resolve to change. Sometimes, we even undergo healing therapies to reconcile the issues. However, our subconscious may not have released the patterns. On the conscious level, we are “different than we used to be” because we hold new thought patterns. On the subconscious level, we have not changed because we hold the same soul memories. The good news is, once we begin employing new thought patterns, the subconscious will eventually alter its memory programs. However, there is usually a lag factor on changing subconscious memory programs, during which time we are still vulnerable to falling into our old habits.

The subconscious has many responsibilities, one of them being memory. We have no memory at the conscious level. Our memory sits at the subconscious level, and our conscious must dip into the subconscious archives to recall past memories. In fact, amnesia occurs when someone’s subconscious separates from their conscious based on a traumatic event they do not wish to recall. The subconscious is like an obedient puppy. Once it has been trained through a certain set of conditions, it does not easily release those memories. Have you ever tried to re-train a dog? Our dog slipped on a slick floor in a pet store when he was a puppy. If we do not place throw rugs on our kitchen floor, he hovers at the edge of the carpeting, afraid to set foot on the wood, despite our repeated attempts to reassure him he will not slip. In fact, he becomes so nervous that he causes himself to slip which reinforces his fear. Perhaps, we should try crystal broadcasting on our dog! Remember, your subconscious is just like our dog. Once it learns something, it has a difficult time removing it from the memory.

≈≈≈≈≈≈≈≈≈≈≈≈≈≈≈≈

Imagine someone who lives a life that is overshadowed by a low self-image. Events may occur in childhood that cause that person to have poor self-esteem. Maybe, their parents were extremely judgmental, or the person had a physical imperfection like obesity or big ears or nearsighted vision that required very thick glasses for which they were teased. Even if this person addresses his or her low self-esteem in therapy, it does not necessarily mean they have released traumatic memories in their subconscious. Remember, the subconscious manages our archives. In order to delete something from the archives, it must be either experientially or energetically released.

An energetic release is much faster than an experiential release. I have worked with clients who have repeatedly created uncomfortable learning experiences, sometimes throughout multiple lifetimes, because they believe if they undergo the condition enough times they will finally reconcile and release it. An energy release may occur instantaneously or, in the case of clearing my feminine blockage, in a matter of months. The release of energy is critical to the issue resolution since our physical behavior is patterned after our energy field. People who heal from terminal cancer, with or without traditional medical treatment, have somehow altered the core issue that caused their condition. They have reprogrammed their subconscious. Otherwise, they would have the tendency to re create the condition, hence the high re occurrence rate of cancer.

If you feel you have resolved particular issues in your life because you think differently about them, try dowsing with a pendulum or have someone use kinesiology to muscle test you to determine if your subconscious supports your conscious. There are instructions for dowsing in this manual. You will be amazed at what you thought you had cleared when it has not cleared at all! I use a variety of repatterning techniques to assist people in reprogramming their

≈≈≈≈≈≈≈≈≈≈≈≈≈≈≈≈

subconscious. The crystal broadcasting program is one of them.

Crystals are Models

Crystal broadcasting successfully repatterns the subconscious memory because it alters energy at the molecular level. All molecular structures are composed of energy. When we project the vibratory rate of the energy we desire to have into our energy field, it will eventually adopt the new program because the universe is constantly sending matching vibrations. When we broadcast, we are overlaying our current energy state with the model we wish to have. We impose a training program until it is embraced.

Have you ever learned to dance? Initially, an instructor demonstrates the proper steps. You observe the sequence and lock it into your consciousness. Then, you attempt to repeat the sequence your instructor has displayed. Even though your brain "gets it," your feet do not want to comply. Dance instruction is based on repetition. After attempting to copy the model many times, you are finally able to effortlessly replicate your instructor. In fact, you do not have to consciously determine which foot should be placed in which position because your subconscious has entered it into memory. You are on automatic pilot as you dance, enjoying the movement rather than forcing your feet through the steps. You have BECOME the model.

Broadcasting is just like dance instruction. First, you must have a model for the objective or new state you wish to attain. The model clearly defines the parameters of your objective. This model is written on the Resolution Sheet. The crystal is placed on top of the model, and it acts as the broadcasting device that submits your request to the universe, 24 hours a day, 7 days a week. The Universal Symbol holds the codes for the desired state, enabling the crystal to submit something to the universe that can be interpreted. If you are an excitable person and you desire to reduce your stress level by resonating with calmness, it is much easier to use “calcite” as a model for calmness rather than trying to create the vibration in a system where it does not currently reside. Broadcasting is similar to using a metronome when learning to play the piano. The player can quickly achieve the correct tempo for the music by following the tick-tock of the metronome. Although the piano student can also learn the tempo through free-flow practice, the student is likely to adopt the correct tempo more quickly by following a cadence model. When you broadcast, you create your personal cadence model.

Often, we desire new behaviors. But, after years of displaying undesirable behaviors, we develop habits that create the vibrations under which we tend to operate. In order to alter these vibrations, we must first desire to change. Once the desire has been initiated, we enter the change process. However, I have seen people work on their New Year's resolutions, only to experience defeat, repeating the same resolutions year after year without permanently implementing the change. Ultimately, they throw up their hands in frustration and make statements like “You can't teach an old dog new tricks,” or “You just have to accept me the way I am”. Change is difficult when we do not use a model. Without a model, we have no point of reference for the new behavior we wish to adopt. Once the desire for change has occurred, we can expedite the process and experience greater success by employing crystals as models.

The Crystal Broadcasting Process

There are three items needed to broadcast with crystals, specifically: 1) a Resolution Sheet; 2) the corresponding crystal that reflects the items listed on the Resolution Sheet; and 3) the Universal Symbol.

≈≈≈≈≈≈≈≈≈≈≈≈≈≈≈≈

Follow the steps outlined below when broadcasting via crystals.

1. Begin by creating a Resolution Sheet. Divide a piece of unlined white paper into two columns by drawing a line down the center of the page, from top to bottom. Or, you can make a photocopy of the Resolution Sheet in the appendix and insert your personal information.

2. Write your full name and birth date at the top of the Resolution Sheet in your own handwriting.

3. Title the right column "Prior Condition", and the left column "New Condition". Your right side is your transmitting side, and your left side is your receiving side. You want to release your unwanted toxic behavior patterns from the right, and receive the upgraded energy from the left. Notice that the current energy you wish to eliminate is titled "Prior Condition" instead of "Current Condition". When you submit requests to Spirit, it is more effective to proffer the desirable state, or you run the risk of continuing to vibrate with the undesirable state. From this point forward, you no longer want to focus on your undesirable behavior. The faster you take your attention away from it, the sooner it disappears.

4. Determine the blockage you wish to clear and list it in the right column under "Prior Condition". Maybe, an issue has surfaced from a session with a therapist such as the need to clear your fear of personal communication, replacing it with the ability for intimate communication. Or, you might have visited a healing practitioner who has identified a blockage in your heart due to a past life where you watched loved ones exiled or put to death, and you want to open your heart to its full capacity. Perhaps, a recent marital counseling session has highlighted the judgment you exhibit

toward your spouse, and you wish to replace judgment with unconditional acceptance. Or, maybe you have lived with the fear of flying in airplanes your entire life and wish to change it prior to your trip to Europe. Be very specific about the obstacle you are releasing. It is important to uncover the emotional discord behind the obstacle rather than citing the condition. For example, fear of flying is the symptom. But, assuming you are not the pilot, a loss of control (because you are not flying the plane) may be the emotional problem underlying the fear. Broadcasting will be faster and more effective when you cut to the core concern.

5. Once you have identified your blockage, focus entirely on that specific issue. Naturally, you can use crystal broadcasting to address a myriad of issues. However, you can only select one theme per Resolution Sheet since you are matching your condition with the vibration of a specific crystal. Although you can only select one theme to resolve per crystal, there may be sub-areas that are part of the main theme. Be sure to identify all of the related areas and list those as well. If you are clearing judgment, you may also have sub-issues like rigidity that you may wish to clear, perhaps replacing rigidity with flexibility. Or, you may become anxious when you are critical and you prefer to relax. Be sure to include all of the undesirable outcomes that result from the barrier.

6. It is feasible to use a clear quartz crystal if you do not wish to utilize dowsing or check the charts to determine which crystal best matches your blockage. A quartz crystal acts like an all-purpose broadcaster, enabling you to resolve any condition on the Resolution Sheet. However, the quartz crystal lacks specificity. It is a good broadcaster. But, broadcasting is all that it can do. When you select a crystal that holds a similar energy to your

≈≈≈≈≈≈≈≈≈≈≈≈≈≈≈≈

desired resolution, you are accomplishing two things at the same time. Obviously, you are broadcasting, and you are also holding the energy of the desired resolution in the "frozen" energy of the crystal. A matching crystal shortens the time frame needed for clearing.

7. After you have listed your undesirable traits in the right column under "Prior Condition", you will list the corresponding desirable traits in the left column under "New Condition". For example, if you have "judgment" on the right side, you might place "acceptance" on the left side. It is VERY IMPORTANT to list only positive statements. Do NOT list the positive intention in a negative format, e.g., not fearful, not powerless. There is a universal condition called the Law of Attraction. Energy always seeks similar vibrations, and the universe may interpret your resistance to NOT wanting a particular condition as a signal that you vibrate with the unwanted situation. The universe is "reading" energy, so it might match your intensity level with something you no longer want. Returning to the example of "judgment," you would not list "non-judgmental" in the left column. However, you might list positive conditions like "acceptance", "agreeable", or "neutral". If you have difficulty determining positive attributes for negative conditions, you may wish to purchase Carol Truman's book *Feelings Buried Alive Never Die...* which contains an alphabetical list of negative emotional conditions and their corresponding positive conditions. You can order her book from Olympus Distributing, PO Box 4218, St. George, UT, 84771, 1-800-531-3180.

8. Next, you need to determine which crystal to use. You can refer to the charts included in this book, and match your condition to the identified crystal for resolution of that blockage. Or, you can use a pendulum to dowse the alphabetical lists to

determine the optimal crystal. Instructions for dowsing are included. Use discernment if you decide to purchase a book that contains alphabetical lists of crystals and the particular healing properties for each crystal. Several times I read the author's interpretation of a particular crystal and assumed it was the appropriate crystal to use. However, after dowsing with my pendulum, I discovered there were better choices. If you do not wish to learn dowsing, you can use the lists provided in this book that outline some of the broadcasting capabilities for specific crystals.

9. Once you have determined which crystal to use, you need to procure it. There are several retail sources listed in the appendix. You do not need to purchase a large or perfect specimen. For example, I needed to purchase ten sapphires for a workshop. A local rock shop had tiny, uncut sapphires. Although they were not pretty and, in fact, did not even look like sapphires, I was able to purchase ten un-cut stones, about one-quarter inch in diameter, for one dollar each. These were equally effective. You do not need a large crystal to broadcast since the molecular structure is similar, regardless of size.

10. Sometimes crystals are mixed. If you are unable to find a pure specimen, use a pendulum to dowse to determine if the presence of other crystalline structures will interfere with the broadcasting. Most of the time, the presence of the other structures is ignored since the Resolution Sheet has specified what needs to be addressed. However, sometimes the presence of another crystal acts counter-productively to clearing a specific blockage. If you are unable to find a pure specimen, you may need to search for an alternative crystal. If you cannot find an appropriate alternative crystal, check the essential oils or Bach Flower remedies to determine if any of

≈≈≈≈≈≈≈≈≈≈≈≈≈≈≈≈

these homeopathic formulations can be used. You will need to place a clear quartz crystal next to an essential oil or Bach Flower remedy to conduct the broadcasting.

11. After purchasing your crystal, you need to clear it. Or, if you already own a crystal and have been using it for other purposes, you should also clear it. Crystals have the ability to retain energy from the environment. You need to ensure your crystal is clear. There are many ways to clear crystals. For example, mix one tablespoon of sea salt with one cup of water and leave the crystal in that mixture for twenty-four hours. If you purchase large crystals, mix more salt water, retaining the ratio. Do not use regular table salt since sea salt holds purification properties that are not present in table salt based on the crystalline structure of the salt. Sea salt is sold in health food stores as well as many traditional supermarkets. If your crystal is in a jewelry setting, and you do not wish to place it in water, you may use pure salt. You can also place the crystal in the sun for several days.

12. After you have cleared your crystal, you might want to ask permission to use it for broadcasting. Ask to please grant you permission to use it for healing, just like the Native American's ask permission of the land for its use. This is a sign of respect and partnership, and your crystal will actually perform better for you.

13. Program the crystal by placing it in the palm of your left hand. Place your right hand, palm up, underneath your left hand. Read the list of "New Conditions" the crystal will be broadcasting, stating (you can paraphrase) "Please act as a model and broadcaster on my behalf for these new behaviors I am adopting, specifically (READ NEW CONDITIONS)". Be sure to read the new

conditions ALOUD. When you create the Resolution Sheet, select the crystal, and program it, you conduct tangible activities. When you enact a tangible event, you gain the attention of the subconscious and communicate the importance of the event.

14. After you have completed your Resolution Sheet and have procured and cleared your crystal, place the Resolution Sheet on top of the Universal Symbol. A copy of the Universal Symbol is included in the appendix for photocopying. Or, if you desire a color version of the Universal Symbol, you can visit www.annebrewer.com and print a copy. Store your broadcasting set-up on a shelf in your closet or in a drawer to minimize disturbing it during the broadcasting period. Although it does not hurt anything to move your papers and crystal, it is best to leave it in a quiet place to do its work.

15. After placing the Universal Symbol under the Resolution Sheet, put your crystal on the LEFT column entitled "New Condition". Be sure to position it on the left side because it contains the energy you wish to receive. You are using your crystal to model the NEW conditions, not the prior conditions.

16. The time frame for resolution varies. Some Resolution Sheets are complete in two weeks. Others are still percolating after four months. I use the pendulum to dowse the required time frame when I set the crystal on the Resolution Sheet. I ask, "Given everything that exists at this time, will it take more than a month for this crystal to complete the broadcasting process for the new conditions?" If I receive a "yes", I continue to expand the time period, asking "Will it take more than two months?", and so forth, until I receive a "no" answer. If I determine the broadcasting will be completed before the end of one month, I

shorten the time period, asking "Will it take more than three weeks?", "Two weeks?", and so forth, until I have identified the time frame.

17. Remember, we live in a free choice/free will world, and sometimes unforeseen events occur that alter estimated time frames. For this reason, you should dowse at the end of the time period to determine if the broadcasting process was completed according to the anticipated schedule. If not, leave the crystal on the Resolution Sheet.

18. When the broadcasting process is complete, it is a good idea to clear the crystal of the items it was broadcasting. Besides, you may want to use it for something else. If you have used a clear quartz crystal, you may want to employ it to broadcast a new list of conditions. Use the steps outlined in #11 to clear the crystal.

Summary of the Crystal Broadcasting Process

1. Write your full name and birth date at the top of a Resolution Sheet.

2. Title the right column "Prior Condition", and the left column "New Condition".

3. Determine the blockage you wish to clear and list it in the right column under "Prior Condition". Identify all of the sub-categories of unwanted behaviors and list those as well.

4. After listing your undesirable traits in the right column under "Prior Condition", list the corresponding desirable trait in the left column under "New Condition". It is VERY IMPORTANT to only list positive statements.

5. Determine which crystal to use. You can refer to the charts included in this book, and match your

≈≈≈≈≈≈≈≈≈≈≈≈≈≈≈≈

condition to the identified crystal for that blockage. Or, dowse the alphabetical lists to determine the optimal crystal. Or, use a quartz crystal to clear any blockage.

6. Procure the crystal.

7. If you are unable to find a pure specimen, use a pendulum to dowse to determine if the presence of other crystalline structures will interfere with the broadcasting. If so, and you cannot find an appropriate alternative crystal, place a clear quartz crystal next to an essential oil or Bach Flower remedy that matches the desired conditions.

8. Clear the crystal. Mix one tablespoon of sea salt with one cup of water, and leave the crystal in that mixture for twenty-four hours. Or, place the crystal in the sun for several days.

9. Honor the crystal by asking permission to use it for broadcasting.

10. Program the crystal by placing it in the palm of your left hand. Place your right hand, palm up, underneath your left hand. Read the list of new conditions that the crystal will be broadcasting ALOUD.

11. Place the Resolution Sheet on top of the Universal Symbol.

12. Put your crystal on the LEFT column entitled "New Condition".

13. When the broadcasting process is complete, clear the crystal of the items it was broadcasting.

≈≈≈≈≈≈≈≈≈≈≈≈≈≈≈≈

Broadcasting with Homeopathics & Essential Oils

Broadcasting can occur through any item that holds a specific molecular structure and works with subtle energy. For example, Bach Flower Essences are homeopathic formulations that heal the non-physical subtle bodies. Homeopathic formulas are extreme dilutions, and they carry a specific molecular frequency. They are designed to alter energy at an etheric level by corresponding with the energy being cleared. Like crystals, they hold specific energy patterns so they are perfect candidates for broadcasting.

These essences, and the books that interpret their specific functions, are available in most health food stores. You can determine which Bach Flower Essence addresses the area you wish to heal and purchase that particular formulation. While you are ingesting the drops, you can store the bottle on a Resolution Sheet that addresses the new conditions you desire. Then, place a clear quartz crystal next to the homeopathic frequency to enable the vibration to be broadcast. Be sure to use a clear quartz crystal because other crystals have very specific vibrations that might conflict with what you are transmitting. The bottle of homeopathic solution will hold the vibration you want, reiterating and reinforcing the conditions you have written on your Resolution Sheet. You will clear issues in a shorter time period since you can ingest the drops in addition to broadcasting.

Essential oils are also capable of broadcasting. People purchase essential oils for healing because the vibration of the oil alters subtle energy. Again, there are many oils available, and there are many publications that define the uses of each oil. Like the Bach Flower Essences, the bottle of essential oil can be placed on a Resolution Sheet that corresponds with the healing properties of the oil. Again, a clear crystal is necessary to complete the broadcasting process.

≈≈≈≈≈≈≈≈≈≈≈≈≈≈≈≈≈

The oil can also be rubbed on the body to move the energy via multiple levels. However, it is important to note that only *natural* essential oils can be used. Broadcasting relies on a natural, not a manmade, vibration.

≈≈≈≈≈≈≈≈≈≈≈≈≈≈≈≈

A sample Resolution Sheet is shown below. A blank one is located in the appendix. Note that all resolutions are sub-categories of the primary negative condition of "impatience."

SAMPLE RESOLUTION SHEET

Name: Anne Brewer

Birth Date: December 12, 1953

New Condition	Prior Condition
1. Patient and loving	1. Impatient
2. Take time to assess situations, consider all aspects of a situation prior to responding	2. Quick to react
3. Remain calm in any situation, stay aligned with true desires regardless of situation	3. Overreact to situations
4. Make positive assumptions, react positively, believe the glass is half full	4. Assume negative outcomes, react negatively, believe the glass is half empty

≈≈≈≈≈≈≈≈≈≈≈≈≈≈≈≈

CHAPTER 3

THE UNIVERSAL SYMBOL

Discovering the Universal Symbol

When I initially began receiving information about crystal broadcasting from Spirit, I knew I needed a translating device for the conditions listed on the Resolution Sheet. Remember, you write the new conditions you desire on the Resolution Sheet and place the crystal on top of the written words. Although the crystal is a broadcasting device, it does not necessarily represent what has been written. You can match the energy of the crystal to the intentions you have written on your Resolution Sheet by selecting the optimal crystal. However, there are nuances that might be lost between the crystal's energy and the written intentions. A symbol was needed that contained a universal language. This symbol would translate all aspects of the desired condition to the universe.

I was perplexed. I knew I needed a symbol, but what symbol was it? What could be so universal that it would contain all of the intentions in the universe? About two weeks passed and I was sharing the broadcasting process with my friend, Dr. Tom Rodman. I explained my dilemma. Fortunately, Tom has studied many esoteric teachings, and he was familiar with sacred geometry. Tom told me to explore the sacred geometrical symbols like the Platonic solids -- symbols that represent the building blocks of matter. In fact, the geometry of form has been proven to be an accurate measure of everything in the universe. Tom also felt I should explore the Flower of Life since it was the basis of sacred geometry teachings.

At the time, I knew very little about sacred geometry. I had tried to read Robert Lawlor's and Dan Winter's work, but I experienced difficulty because of my weak math background. I decided to re-read Gregg Braden's *Awakening to Zero Point* and Val Valerian's *Matrix IV* information on the Flower of Life. Since I had read their work once before, I had an easier time understanding it. I also explored *The Beginner's Guide to Constructing the Universe* by Michael S. Schneider and *The Ancient Secret of the Flower of Life* by Drunvalo Melchizedek.

As I read about sacred geometry, it became clear that I was to use the Flower of Life as the Universal Symbol since it represents the creation of life. However, Spirit was very insistent about using a rendition rather than the actual Flower of Life. I was told to extend it "five levels". I would not gain insight into what that meant or why that was necessary for some time. In order to understand how I developed the Universal Symbol, I need to share some basic information about the Flower of Life symbol.

The Flower of Life

The Flower of Life (fig. a) is a geometric symbol composed of nineteen interlocking circles enclosed in two concentric rings.

FLOWER OF LIFE (a)

This symbol holds the codes of creation. The ancient Egyptian deity, Thoth, referenced this code as the

Flower of Life in his writings called *The Emerald Tablets*. However, the Flower of Life symbol is not confined to Egypt. The Flower of Life, and patterns based on it, known as the Tree of Life, the Fruit of Life, and the Seed of Life, have been found in ancient sites all over the world.

The Flower of Life appears in the Osirion Temple complex in Egypt. It is believed this site was used as a spiritual school approximately thirteen thousand years ago. As with many powerful spiritual teachings, the information was kept hidden, passing from initiate to initiate so the power was not abused. Given the creation codes housed in the Flower of Life symbol, it is understandable that the Osirion Temple is also called the Temple of Resurrection based on the Egyptian legend that Osiris' wife, Isis, brought the severed portions of Osiris' body to this site to be re-endowed with life, i.e., re-created.

The Flower of Life contains all of the mathematical sequences that represent the codes of creation. The shape was created when Spirit moved in a sphere pattern to manifest creation. It begins with a single circle since the circle represents unity. In order for unity to become many, the circle needs to extend beyond itself. The circle represents consciousness, and its awareness is confined to what it is, until it ventures beyond what it is. When consciousness expands beyond what it knows, it looks outside itself.

Initial consciousness exists as a sphere because Spirit became aware of itself by rotating in all directions on its axis as it looked up, down, back, front, left, and right. The space within the sphere was the only world that consciousness knew since it was its entire existence. However, at some point, consciousness grew bored with what it knew. It desired to expand beyond the spherical limits of what it already knew. It wished to move into the unknown and incorporate new experiences into its sphere of existence.

≈≈≈≈≈≈≈≈≈≈≈≈≈≈≈≈

Therefore, it went to the very edge of its world and extended itself beyond its knowing into the next void, i.e., that which it did not know. When it projected its knowing into the unknown, it created a sphere the same size as the first one. It is identical in size because consciousness' ability to project into the void is always the same. The intersection of the two spheres creates a form called a vesica piscis (fig. b), pronounced like the astrological sign Pisces.

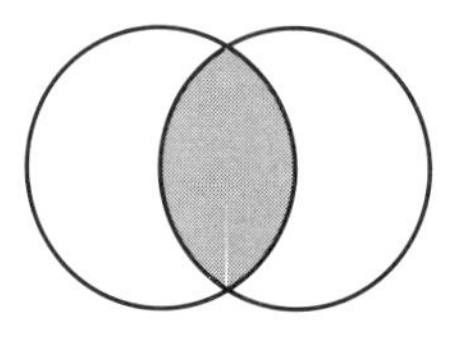

VESICA PISCIS (b)

A vesica piscis is formed when a circle is bisected by another circle of exactly the same size. Once one circle expands to two, it creates a dyad. The dyad, then, is the doorway between one (unity) and many (expanded consciousness). The vesica piscis has attracted the attention of mathematicians, artists, and architects throughout history. In Christian cultures, it represents the fish which is the symbol for Christ. Moslem arches and cathedral doorways were designed using two intersecting circles and the vesica piscis, with the intention of representing the passage from duality to unity (i.e., the return to the original state of consciousness) as one passes from the outside world into the inner spiritual domain.

The vesica piscis is the fundamental vessel for the creation process. It is the opening from which the geometric shapes and forms of our universe are born. The triangle, square, and pentagon are the first three shapes that emerge from the vesica piscis (fig. c).

≈≈≈≈≈≈≈≈≈≈≈≈≈≈≈≈

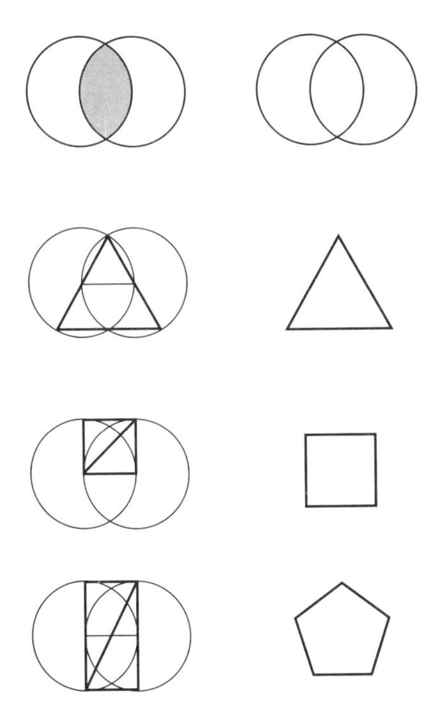

TRIANGLE, SQUARE, & PENTAGON IN VESICA PISCIS (c)

These three shapes contain everything necessary to generate the five Platonic solids. Architects and engineers spend time studying the five shapes because they are the basis of structures. The five Platonic solids are the Tetrahedron (4 triangular faces), Hexahedron or Cube (6 square faces), Octahedron (8 triangular faces), Dodecahedron (12 pentagonal faces), and Icosohedron (20 triangular faces).

The Platonic solids are the only five possible equal divisions of three-dimensional space. These solids are the only three-dimensional shapes that fit perfectly within a sphere and present an identical view in all

≈≈≈≈≈≈≈≈≈≈≈≈≈≈≈≈

directions, no matter how you turn them. The faces of these forms consist of either triangles, squares, or pentagons. No other flat shape, alone, will enclose a volume without gaps. Their order and symmetry bespeak of Divine composition that overlays the seemingly chaotic view of nature.

Variations of these five shapes are virtually endless in nature. The Platonic solids are the basis for the shapes of all crystals. The measurements involved in these shapes have also been found to be identical to spatial representations of musical harmonies. Given this fact, crystals might even be considered "frozen music" holding the proportions of musical intervals in the relationships of their corners, edges, and faces. It is the frozen nature of a crystal that enables it to "hold" the resolution you wish to broadcast.

The equilateral triangle is the first surface area that emerges from the vesica piscis. A triangle is symbolic of relationship and balance. In many situations, opposites are balanced by a third element that reconciles the conflict. Triangles are necessary to create self-supporting structures. Unlike any other shape, the three sides of a triangle resolve opposite tensions into one stable whole that does not require support from elsewhere. Ancient philosophers were struck by the harmony of the vesica piscis' space which generates triangles by its natural points.

Three points define a flat surface, but a fourth point is needed to experience depth. When a fourth point is introduced into the mix, three more shapes emerge through the vesica piscis, specifically the square, the cube, and the tetrahedron. The tetrahedron commonly occurs in organic and inorganic chemistry and in sub-microscopic structures. Its geometry is seen in methane, ethane, and ammonium, the basis of the amino acids or building blocks of life.

≈≈≈≈≈≈≈≈≈≈≈≈≈≈≈≈

The pentagon, the last of the surface areas that create the Platonic solids, also emerges from the vesica piscis. Many living forms display the geometry of the pentagon in their structure. The overall design of a plant leaf fits within a stretched or compressed pentagon. The flower of every edible fruit has five petals. The power of the pentagon is seen in the ability of vegetation to regenerate a replica of itself from a portion of the original. For example, some leaves will root when put in soil. Thus, we have moved from the building blocks of life to life itself.

Based on sacred geometry, all creation is contained in a vesica piscis. In fact, the vesica piscis is the Egyptian glyph for the "creator". It is no coincidence that the Flower of Life is made up entirely of the vesica piscis. Remember, consciousness has traveled to the edge of its world and created the first vesica piscis. At some point, consciousness must expand since it is only happy when experiencing creation. Once again, consciousness moves to outside the second circle and projects a new sphere, pushing above, below, around, and about itself. Each time a new sphere is formed, more and more information unfolds and more and more creation patterns emerge. Consciousness continues to expand awareness by repeating the projecting action.

A six petal flower results when consciousness completes one full turn from its original starting point. It is interesting to compare that six petal flower to the six days of Genesis in the Old Testament. The Bible says that creation was formed in six days. Could the Flower of Life pattern be the beginning of creation?

If the creation codes are present in the six petal formation, why does the Flower of Life contain nineteen interlocking circles? As explained, the first rotation of circles depicts the six days of Genesis. Once the Genesis pattern is completed, consciousness continues to move to new spheres of experience, completing a second rotation. This cluster of spheres is called the Egg of Life (fig. d).

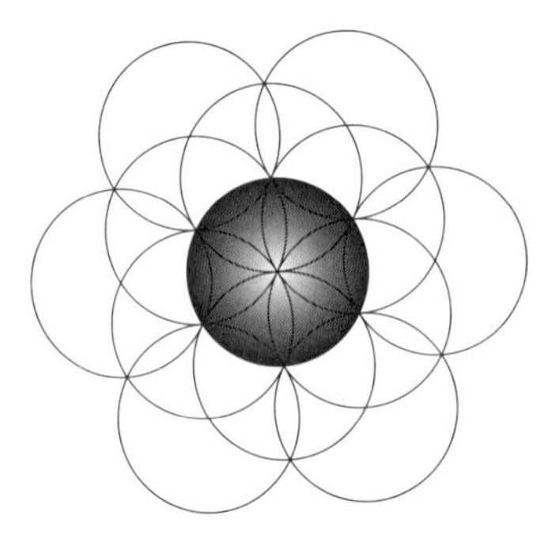

EGG OF LIFE (d)

The Egg of Life contains creation codes for the physical body. In fact, the Egg of Life depicts the division of cells that occur during the formation of a fetus. From the Egg of Life, consciousness continues its third rotation to create the nineteen interlocking circles of the Flower of Life (fig. e), the symbol that is frequently found at ancient sites like the Osirian Temple.

FLOWER OF LIFE (e)

Notice that the exterior circles are not complete. Instead, they are cut off and enclosed by a double circle. Some believe the Flower of Life is abbreviated because the complete figure contains mystical information that was not considered safe for public

≈≈≈≈≈≈≈≈≈≈≈≈≈≈≈≈

knowledge. It would be like advertising a fool-proof formula for acing the stock market or ruining the economy on the Internet. This information is disclosed when finishing off the incomplete circles. The completed drawing depicts the Fruit of Life (figure f).

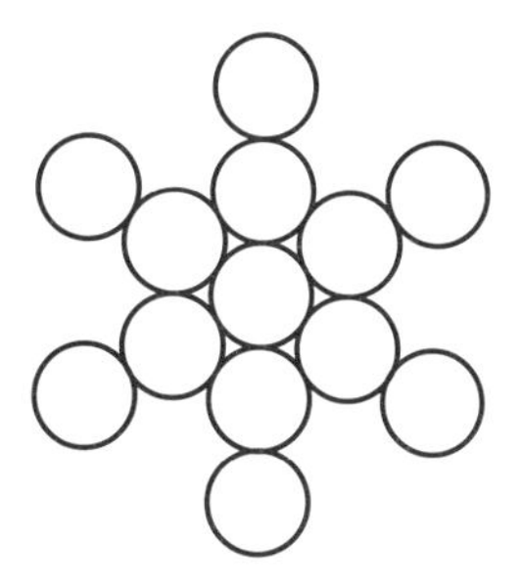

FRUIT OF LIFE (f)

The Flower of Life is the basis for the Fruit of Life. The Fruit of Life is an extension of the nineteen interlocking circles. It completes the incomplete circles at the edge of the Flower of Life, creating the most sacred geometrical configuration. It is called the Fruit of Life because it is the result, the fruit, which comprises reality. The Fruit of Life is depicted by thirteen circles within the expanded Flower of Life.

≈≈≈≈≈≈≈≈≈≈≈≈≈≈≈≈

The pattern of thirteen circles is one of the most sacred forms. By superimposing straight lines over the Fruit of Life, thirteen patterns are created, including the Egg of Life and the Fruit of Life. These thirteen patterns contain mathematical codes that represent everything in existence, in our universe and other universes. One of these thirteen patterns is called Metatron's Cube, an important informational system that contains numerous creation blueprints.

Examination of the Fruit of Life indicates that, like the Flower of Life, the arc of each circle bisects the circle adjacent to it at exactly the one-half point, passing through the center of that circle. Thus, each of the circles are related to each other, having the same diameter, with each edge sharing the space of one-half that of its neighboring circle. Where does the pattern start, and where does it end? It reproduces itself again and again. Yet, the entire pattern also exists within each sphere. This relates to the holographic nature of our cells whereby every single cell can reproduce our entire body since our genetic code is contained in each cell.

Our holographic make-up has already been proven in England with sheep cloning experiments. Just like a single cell that houses the genetic code for our entire body, each sphere or cell in the Fruit of Life is whole and complete while also forming a component of something much more than it can be alone. This pattern symbolizes a tree which yields a flower which yields a seed which yields a tree again. The miracle of creation represented by this pattern occurs year after year. We take it for granted. However, without the type of sequence represented by an acorn becoming a tree that yields acorns which drop to the ground and germinate more trees, we would cease to exist.

The Fruit of Life appears to be the structure or grid for all atomic structures. Thinking back to the graphic depiction of the atoms studied in high school chemistry, there were very specific patterns for each element on the atomic table. Particles of matter conformed to specific configurations. The Fruit of Life is the structure that particles follow. It is the "force" that appears to hold the particles of an atom together.

Greg Braden, author of *Awakening to Zero Point*, has plotted the configuration of essential amino acids like Glycine, Alanine, and Leucine within the Fruit of Life. In addition to the essential amino acids, the Fruit of Life contains:

- The Platonic solids
- Biological programs that orchestrate the direction and growth rate of life
- Ratios of males to females in unregulated populations
- Branching patterns of trees and plants
- Branching patterns of electrical discharges in the atmosphere
- Proportions of geometric fields of energy radiating within and beyond the human body

Thus, the creation template is contained in the Fruit of Life. The blueprint through which everything in existence was created, without exception, is based on the Fruit of Life. The shape of our body, the color of our eyes and all biological life forms, all crystal structures, all mathematical formulas -- basically everything in existence is based on this image.

The Universal Symbol

The Universal Symbol used for crystal broadcasting is a derivative of the Flower of Life. It is *not* the Flower of Life. When I read about the Flower of Life, I thought it consisted of an unlimited number of vesica piscis. I did not understand the true Flower of Life consisted of nineteen interlocking circles, and the outermost circles are cut off, i.e., incomplete. I contacted my artist friend, Susan Tower, and asked her to help me create the symbol I needed to use. Susan is an accomplished commercial artist, and she is an exceptional spiritual artist. Susan uses her psychic energy to create beautiful spirit guide pictures, and I knew she could receive whatever guidance I was unable to give her directly when developing the Universal Symbol.

I explained my objectives to Susan. I told her about the Flower of Life and how my guides had instructed me to "take it out five levels". I told her I did not yet know why five levels were important. Susan laughed when she heard what I wanted because she had just developed a game using the Flower of Life symbol and already had it in her computer. She said she would develop some prototypes to show me.

When she returned with her prototypes, I was initially surprised. She showed me the Flower of Life symbol she had developed with a tissue overlay that counted the levels (fig. g). The design was different than I envisioned. As I gazed at Susan's interpretation and recognized its validity based on her rationale, I realized how many designs might have been created by expanding the vesica piscis of the Flower of Life by five levels.

I felt Susan had received the correct information because she showed me a color version she created. By expanding the Flower of Life symbol according to her interpretation of five levels, she had just enough circles to depict the colors of the seven primary chakras. Her color version began with a red core, followed by a ring of orange spheres, yellow spheres, green spheres, blue spheres, indigo spheres, and, finally, violet spheres. The color version is depicted on the cover of this book and can be printed on a color printer by accessing www.annebrewer.com.

≈≈≈≈≈≈≈≈≈≈≈≈≈≈≈≈

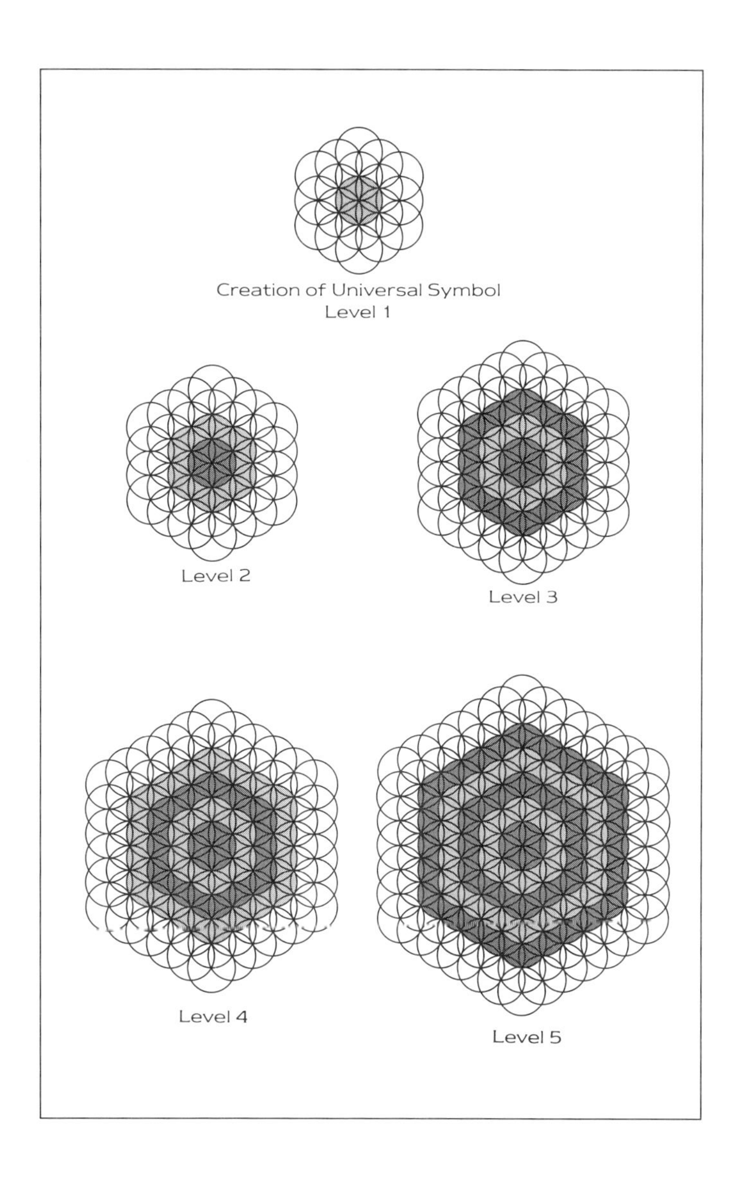

FIVE LEVELS ACCORDING TO SUSAN (g)

≈≈≈≈≈≈≈≈≈≈≈≈≈≈≈≈

In viewing the colored Universal Symbol, I knew I had obtained exactly what my guides desired since it represented the seven basic energy centers of our existence. Essentially, all aspects of our physical and spiritual well-being in addition to the universal creation codes are entrenched in the Universal Symbol design as follows.

1. Root chakra -- Red
   - Will to live
2. Sexual chakra -- Orange
   - Giving and receiving pleasure, creativity and manifestation derived from desire
3. Solar plexus chakra -- Yellow
   - General health in body/mind/spirit and emotional balance
4. Heart chakra -- Green
   - Giving and receiving love, unconditional love
5. Throat chakra -- Blue
   - Communication, self-image
6. Brow chakra -- Indigo
   - Visionary abilities, connection to Universal Truth
7. Crown chakra -- Violet
   - Self-empowerment, pathway to the Divine, spiritual center

In addition to representing the seven primary energy centers of mankind, the Universal Symbol also contains our visible color spectrum. Look at any rainbow, and you will see the seven colors that comprise our visible color spectrum, i.e., red, orange, yellow, green, blue, indigo, and violet. Although the seven colors appear to be differentiated, they actually represent unity. Isaac Newton performed an experiment with a glass prism and a shaft of sunlight in a darkened room. Newton observed that when a shaft of sunlight entered the prism, it emerged as a rainbow. He determined that sunlight, appearing as white light, represents the whole because it is a mix of many colors that overlap. When the individual colors emerge from the sun, they blend into white. The prism refracts the sunlight, proving white light is the blend of all colors.

Thus, the seven colors contain everything when blended together. Yet, white is nothing. It is all colors, but it looks like the absence of color or "no color". Just like consciousness that existed nowhere or in the void until it started to explore outside itself, the combination of all colors create a visible void (white on white), but when each component reveals itself, masterpieces are possible.

After seeing Susan's design, Spirit shared the reason for the seven circles in the Universal Symbol beyond the obvious linkage to the seven primary chakra centers of the physical body. Seven is the final number or stage that is reached prior to a new event. In the case of the seven colors of the rainbow, the next vibration creates colors in another spectrum that are invisible to human sight. The seven white keys on the piano, the Dorian musical scale, consists of seven notes (EDCBAGF) that must be played before a new octave is reached. The process of cell division, called mitosis, occurs in seven stages before a single cell splits into two cells. There are seven days in a week, then we begin the next week.

Thus, seven is the transition point to new experiences such as the beginning of a new color vibration, musical octave, or cell division. Of all the numbers, it appears seven can best represent the firmly entrenched habits and patterns we create when we repeat the same toxic behavior over and over again. Yet, it also represents that point of no return when we bridge to the next experience, the one for which all prior experiences have prepared us. The Universal Symbol represents our current behavior. It also holds the promise of the behavior that results when moving

≈≈≈≈≈≈≈≈≈≈≈≈≈≈≈≈

away from our well-defined, current level of consciousness and entering something new.

I wondered why the Fruit of Life was not capable of representing the Universal Symbol for crystal broadcasting since it contains the creation codes of the universe. In other words, the All should be inherent in the Fruit of Life if it represents the blueprint for every color, every chakra, every experience. Spirit explained it -- as long as the Universal Symbol contained the Fruit of Life, it had the ability to translate all blueprints. In other words, any additional circles beyond the Fruit of Life configuration did not interfere with its translation capacity. By extending the circles to incorporate the seven primary energy centers of our physical existence which is the All of our experience, both physical and spiritual, it becomes pertinent to the types of resolutions we wish to obtain. Yet, it also contains the Fruit of Life.

Why the Universal Symbol is Open-ended

I also was curious about the "unfinished" edges in the Universal Symbol, unlike the Flower of Life that was surrounded by two circles (fig. h).

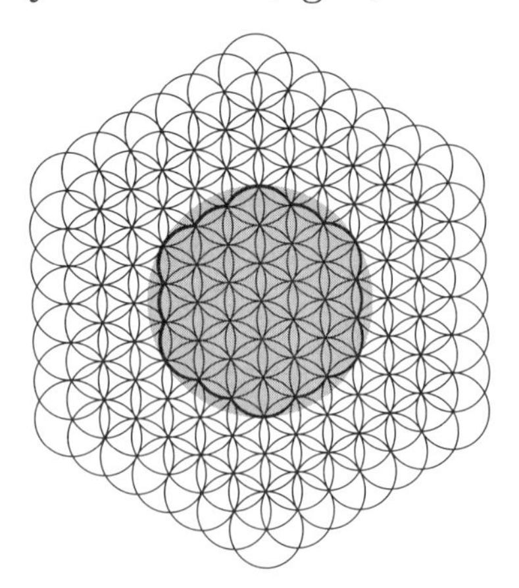

FLOWER OF LIFE INSIDE UNIVERSAL SYMBOL (h)

≈≈≈≈≈≈≈≈≈≈≈≈≈≈≈≈

According to Spirit, the open-ended format of the Universal Symbol enables creation to continue to unfold. Instead of limiting growth to what we can define at our current level of understanding, it enables creation beyond our paradigms. The Universal Symbol represents the *unlimited potential* of creation by remaining open-ended. It embodies everything we can be, beyond our concept of what is. It by-passes any limitations we might have imposed on our growth due to ignorance.

Spend some time observing the Universal Symbol before you use it for broadcasting. You can easily become lost in its seemingly endless interplay of vesica piscis. Feel the power that is held in the symbol and know that it is working on your behalf, interpreting your intentions for healing. Tap into the secrets that ancient societies held regarding the power of this symbol as you use it to broadcast your resolutions.

≈≈≈≈≈≈≈≈≈≈≈≈≈≈≈≈

UNIVERSAL SYMBOL

A color version depicting the 7 chakras is available at www.annebrewer.com. Click on the *Crystal Broadcasting* book cover and print on a color printer.

≈≈≈≈≈≈≈≈≈≈≈≈≈≈≈≈≈

CHAPTER 4

MODELING ABILITIES OF POPULAR CRYSTALS

Crystals and Conditions

Although information is included on how to use a pendulum to determine the optimal crystal for broadcasting, everyone may not wish to learn to dowse. Therefore, a list has been provided of popular crystals and the conditions they model. The following tables identify the crystal. Next to each crystal, there is a summary of the positive emotional and physical conditions modeled by the crystal.

Both the emotional and physical imprints that you no longer desire are located in the blueprint of your subtle bodies, e.g., etheric, emotional, mental, astral. Once the crystal starts broadcasting, the imprint begins to change as the new positive energy overrides the existing negative energy. The shift from the old to the new energy takes time. Remember, the crystal is holding your new intention, 24 hours a day, 7 days a week. As you project the upgraded vibration, the universe starts to match that vibration with corresponding energy. Ultimately, you make the shift to holding the new energy on your own. Then, the crystal is no longer needed.

An emotional shift is more easily achieved than a physical one. The physical has been entrenched in the cellular memory of your body, and it simply takes more time to change. It is also important to note that the physical condition is much more likely to improve if the underlying, corresponding emotional condition has been addressed and cleared.

Plus, after the energy has been upgraded, there has to be conscious choice on your part. In other words, you must consciously opt to make new choices. The crystal alters your energy blueprint, which is the first step to experiencing emotional and physical change. The new blueprint eliminates the "tug" you have experienced as your subconscious drives you to unwanted behaviors. However, you must take responsibility for new choices rather than lapsing into the habitual patterns of the past.

Sometimes, there is no information under the Physical Conditions column because Spirit did not provide any. The metaphysical crystal reference books identify the physical maladies that each crystal heals. If a blank appears, it means Spirit would not substantiate the published information on the physical healing qualities of these crystals. I recommend you examine this through dowsing with a pendulum since you may obtain different information as it pertains to your own physical system.

Once you determine which crystal you desire to use to assist you in clearing your issue, follow the instructions to initiate the broadcasting process.

≈≈≈≈≈≈≈≈≈≈≈≈≈≈≈≈

Crystal	Emotional Conditions	Physical Conditions
Acanthite	• Protection, safety	• Boosts immune system
Adamite	• Prosperous business • Processing through the heart instead of the mind	• Addresses heart, lung, and throat disorders
Adularia	• Clarity • Work performance	• Addresses parasympathetic nervous system disorders
Aegirine	• Protection from psychic attack • Self-acceptance • True to oneself, self-conviction	• Addresses immune system disorders
Agate	• Analytical capability, precise thinking • Courage, strength, fortitude • Marital fidelity • Self-assurance	• Addresses sight disorders
Ajoite	• Impartiality • Peace within self, self-acceptance • Processing through the heart instead of the mind	• Helps disengage ET implants
Alabaster	• Acceptance	• Addresses heart disorders
Albite	• Clarity • Tact, diplomacy	• Addresses ambulation and eye disorders

≈≈≈≈≈≈≈≈≈≈≈≈≈≈≈≈≈

Crystal	Emotional Conditions	Physical Conditions
Alexandrite	• Calm, peaceful • Self-esteem	• Addresses nervous system, pancreas, spleen, and testicle disorders
Almandine	• Peace when contemplating • Profound love	• Addresses liver and pancreas disorders • Increases physical vitality
Alurgite	• Awakens the senses • Perspective	• Addresses elimination system disorders • Alleviates tension, stress
Amazonite	• Creativity, imagination • Love communication • Peace of mind	• Increases metabolism • Soothes muscle spasms • Addresses nervous system and neurological disorders
Amber	• Manifestation • Past life recall • Soothes	• Addresses bladder, heart, kidney, nerve, and throat disorders
Amethyst	• Freedom • Psychic abilities • Spiritual awareness	• Cleanses toxins from blood • Reduces fatigue • Addresses skeletal structure and teeth disorders
Ammonite	• Relaxation • Stability	• Addresses limb disorders

≈≈≈≈≈≈≈≈≈≈≈≈≈≈≈≈

Crystal	Emotional Conditions	Physical Conditions
Ametrine	• Balances male and female qualities	• Removes aura blockages • Balances the electromagnetic energy field
Angelite	• Clear communication	• Addresses throat disorders
Angel Wing Agate	• Clairaudience • Concentration • Kundalini movement	• Reduces infection • Addresses intestinal and lung disorders
Anhydrite	• Acceptance of change	• Addresses throat disorders
Antigorite	• Intuition	• Helps release toxicity
Apache Tear	• Fortunateness • Protection • Psychic abilities • Self-confidence • Success • Willpower	• Increases vitality and strength
Aqua-marine	• Acceptance, tolerance • Love • Serenity/peace • Truth	• Addresses gland and nerve disorders
Aragonite	• Discipline	• Addresses deficiency in Vitamin A and D
Artinite	• Crucial decisions	• Addresses throat disorders
Azurite	• Appreciation of life • Creativity • Decision making	• Improves poor circulation • Increases vitality

≈≈≈≈≈≈≈≈≈≈≈≈≈≈≈≈≈≈

Crystal	Emotional Conditions	Physical Conditions
Barite	• Motivation	• Alleviates addictions • Addresses eye disorders
Beryl	• Love • Psychic abilities • Relationships	• Addresses eye, gland, and liver disorders
Black Agate	• Communication • Grounding, centering	• Addresses ear, nose, throat, intestinal, and vein disorders
Black Opal	• Aligns sexuality with spirituality	• Improves digestion
Bloodstone	• Contentment • Creativity • Inspiration • Living in the "now"	• Improves oxygen-carrying capacity of blood
Bornite	• Curiosity	• Increases adrenaline flow
Botswana Agate	• Creativity • Solutions	• Addresses nervous system disorders
Brazilian Agate	• Strength	• Addresses ligament disorders
Calcite	• Calm, peaceful • Emotional balance • Freedom	• Helps release toxicity
Carnallite	• Expressiveness • Persuasiveness	• Reduces bloating and water retention
Carnelian	• Concentration • Love	• Helps alleviate kidney stones

≈≈≈≈≈≈≈≈≈≈≈≈≈≈≈≈

Crystal	Emotional Conditions	Physical Conditions
Cat's Eye	• Good fortune • Protection • Wealth	• Addresses eye and nervous system disorders
Cerussite	• Composure • Life growth	• Increases vitality during illness
Chalce-dony	• Joy • Protection • Receptivity	• Addresses lactation disorders • Improves mental stability
Chlorite (Group)	• Conciliation • Centered in heart energy	• Helps release toxicity
Chryso-colla	• Femininity • Self-confidence • Understanding of others	• Addresses menstrual cycle disorders
Chryso-prase	• Contented • Self introspection, insight	• Increases fertility
Citrine	• Joys of spirit • Problem solving	• Addresses digestion and thymus gland disorders
Copper	• Vitality	• Improves skin tone and flexibility
Diamond	• Orderly, methodical	• Increases metabolism
Diaspor	• Rejuvenation	• NA
Dioptase	• Emotional stability	• Addresses nervous system disorders

≈≈≈≈≈≈≈≈≈≈≈≈≈≈≈≈

Crystal	Emotional Conditions	Physical Conditions
Emerald	• Emotional stability • Successful love	• Improves the immune system
Fire Agate	• Excellence, best one can be	• Increases energy level
Fluorite	• Creativity • Right brain activity	• Improves immune system
Garnet	• Sacred commitment	• Unblocks restricted energy flow from head to feet
Gold	• Positive mind-set	• Addresses endocrine system disorders
Hematite	• High state of awareness • Inner happiness	• Addresses spine and back disorders
Iolite	• Accuracy within vision • Leadership • Meditation • Vision, perspective	• Strengthens weak physical constitution
Ivory	• Comfortable pace, not too fast or slow • Serenity	• Addresses nervous system disorders
Jade (Green)	• Clarity • Tranquillity	• Helps increase infertility
Jasper	• Unveils subconscious	• Addresses liver disorders
Kunzite	• Calm, peaceful, tranquil	• Addresses chakra system imbalances

≈≈≈≈≈≈≈≈≈≈≈≈≈≈≈≈

Crystal	Emotional Conditions	Physical Conditions
Labra-dorite	• Opens subconscious • Encourages communication between subconscious and conscious	• Increases low metabolism
Laguna Agate	• Intelligence, intellectual pursuits	• Addresses colon disorders
Lapis Lazuli	• Mental balance • Relaxation	• Addresses bone structure disorders
Lavender Quartz	• Joy • Perspective	• NA
Lepidolite	• Calm • Smooth transitions	• NA
Magnetite	• Augments spiritual path • Endurance	• Addresses skin disorders
Malachite	• Contentment, ease • Fidelity, loyalty	• Addresses muscle disorders
Mica	• Energizing	• Increases low energy and improves vitality
Moldavite	• Balance • Grounding	• NA
Moonstone	• Balance • Femininity • Romance	• Helps eliminate female system disorders
Moss Agate	• Unconditional love	• Addresses skin disorders
Mother of Pearl	• Love	• NA

≈≈≈≈≈≈≈≈≈≈≈≈≈≈≈≈

Crystal	Emotional Conditions	Physical Conditions
Morganite	• Creation energy, manifestation through visualization • Open to heart's desires	• Addresses lung disorders
Obsidian	• "Think" with heart instead of intellect	• Surfaces source of malady, reveals core dis-ease
Onyx	• Calming, soothing	• Addresses foot disorders • Reduces infertility
Pearl	• Love • Patience • Peace	• Addresses digestion disorders
Peridot	• Regulates life cycles, eases transitions	• Addresses nervous system disorders
Petrified Wood	• Balance	• Addresses joint disorders
Plume Agate	• Plants ideas	• NA
Polka Dot Agate	• Cheerfulness	• Increases low physical vitality • Addresses skin disorders
Pumice	• Solutions • Surety, certitude	• NA
Purple Sage Agate	• Insight, clear introspection	• Addresses brain and emotional disorders
Pyrite	• Confidence	• Addresses sleep disorders
Quartz (Clear)	• Balance • Oneness, unity	• Improves emotional stability

≈≈≈≈≈≈≈≈≈≈≈≈≈≈≈≈

Crystal	Emotional Conditions	Physical Conditions
Rhodo-chrosite	• Attracting perfect mate • Passion	• Supports balance for optimal health
Rhodonite	• Balances masculine and feminine elements	• Addresses pineal gland disorders
Rhyolite	• Grounding, balance	• NA
Riverstone	• Change	• NA
Rose-Eye Agate	• Gender balance, balance of masculine and feminine	• Assists in detoxing liver or pancreas
Rose Quartz	• Instills love in heart	• Helps reduce male infertility
Rubellite	• Promotes positive emotional response	• Cleanses etheric body
Ruby	• Bliss • Tranquillity	• Addresses addictions
Sapphire	• Emotional balance • Prosperity	• Addresses digestive system disorders
Sardonyx	• Communication between lovers/couples • Joy • Peace	• NA
Selenite	• Rejuvenation	• Increases low energy and improves vitality

≈≈≈≈≈≈≈≈≈≈≈≈≈≈≈≈≈≈

Crystal	Emotional Conditions	Physical Conditions
Silver	• Freedom	• Addresses poor vitamin and mineral absorption
Smoky Quartz	• Relaxation	• NA
Snowflake Obsidian	• Protection	• Addresses root chakra imbalances
Sodalite	• Lightness of heart	• Addresses sexual energy disorders
Sugilite	• Divine love • Resonant love with others and Universe	• Addresses blocked kundalini movement
Sunstone	• Life energy, vital force	• Improves absorption of energy from the sun
Tanzanite	• Aligns visualizations with actualization	• NA
Tiger Eye	• Motivation to succeed • Polarity balance, i.e., left and right brain, male and female gender	• Addresses digestive disorders
Topaz	• Inspiration	• Increases ability to relax
Tourmaline	• Awareness of Universal Truth, insight beyond physical illusions	• Alleviates environmental pollution

≈≈≈≈≈≈≈≈≈≈≈≈≈≈≈≈

Crystal	Emotional Conditions	Physical Conditions
Turquoise	• Longevity • Protection	• NA
White Onyx	• Path and purpose	• NA
Zircon	• Calm, peaceful • Relaxed	• Addresses inner ear disorders

≈≈≈≈≈≈≈≈≈≈≈≈≈≈≈≈

≈≈≈≈≈≈≈≈≈≈≈≈≈≈≈≈≈

CHAPTER 5

ENERGY STATES AND CORRESPONDING CRYSTALS

Conditions and Crystals

Rather than first identifying the crystal, then stating the condition that can be modeled, the following section reverses the order. The tables list the energy state or condition desired and the crystals for modeling each condition.

Although these lists were designed for those who do not wish to dowse, it is recommended that you verify the crystal you select from the list by dowsing since it may not be the optimal match with your particular situation. The dowsing instructions are provided in the next chapter. Additionally, you may find through dowsing that you can use other crystals not specified for that particular condition. Spirit provides answers that apply to the majority of people. These answers may not be an optimal match for your particular energy field which is why you should verify everything for your personal needs.

≈≈≈≈≈≈≈≈≈≈≈≈≈≈≈≈

Energy State	Crystals
Abundance	• Adamite • Cinnabar
Accepting	• Alabaster • Aquamarine
Accurate	• Iolite
Adaptable	• Lepidolite • Purpurite • Riverstone
Adequate	• Spinel
Adventurous	• Chlorite
Agreeable	• Uranophane
Allowing	• Blue Tourmaline
Analytical Thinking	• Agate
Appreciated	• Azurite
Assertive	• Witherite
Assured	• Apache Tear • Chrysocolla • Iolite • Plancheite
Attentive	• Tin
Attracting Mate	• Rhodochrosite
Authentic	• Willemite
Aware	• Blue Lace Agate • Hermatite • Mexican Lace Agate • Tourmaline

≈≈≈≈≈≈≈≈≈≈≈≈≈≈≈≈

Energy State	Crystals
Balanced	• Ametrine • Calcite • Lapis Lazuli • Moldavite, Moonstone • Petrified Wood • Rhodonite • Rhyolite • Sapphire
Beautiful	• Fulgurite
Blessed	• Olivine
Blissful	• Kunzite • Ruby
Brave	• Petrified Wood
Calm	• Alexandrite • Amblygonite • Calcite • Kunzite • Lepidolite • Onyx • Zircon
Capable	• Opal
Caring	• Chrysocolla • Rose Quartz • Verdite
Centered	• Black Agate
Certainty	• Pumice
Cheerful	• Polka Dot Agate
Cherished	• Geode

≈≈≈≈≈≈≈≈≈≈≈≈≈≈≈≈

Energy State	**Crystals**
Clarity	• Adularia • Albite • Chrysopase • Green Jade • Purple Sage Agate
Comfortable	• Ivory • Selenite
Commitment	• Garnet
Communicative	• Amazonite • Angelite • Black Agate • Caledonite • Holly Agate • Sardonyx
Compassionate	• Pyrite • Silver
Compatible	• Emerald • Rhodonite
Complete	• Rhonite
Composed	• Cerussite • Pyrite
Concentration	• Angel Wing Agate • Carnelian
Confident	• Pyrite • Chrysocolla
Congruent	• Aquamarine • Phenacite
Connected	• Flint • Pipestone • Sphene

≈≈≈≈≈≈≈≈≈≈≈≈≈≈≈≈

Energy State	**Crystals**
Contemplative	• Almandine • Purple Sage Agate
Contented	• Bloodstone • Chrysoprase • Malachite
Cooperative	• Opal
Courageous	• Agate
Creative	• Amazonite • Azurite • Bloodstone • Botswana Agate • Fluorite
Curious	• Bornite
Decisive	• Azurite • Ocean Spray Agate
Delighted	• Kernite
Diplomatic	• Ajoite • Albite
Directed	• Shell
Discerning	• London Blue Topaz
Disciplined	• Aragonite
Dynamic	• Champagne Topaz
Eager	• Planerite
Ease (Sense Of)	• Kunzite • Malachite • Peridot • Sodalite

≈≈≈≈≈≈≈≈≈≈≈≈≈≈≈≈

Energy State	**Crystals**
Easy-going	• Gibbsite • Olivine • Pink Angel Wing Dolomite • Sinhalite
Efficient	• Diamond • Shell
Emotionally Open	• Thunderegg
Empowered	• Rhyolite
Energized	• Copper • Mica
Encouraged	• Imperial Topaz
Enlightened	• Iolite • Uranophane
Enthusiastic	• Spinel
Excellence	• Fire Agate
Expressive	• Carnallite
Excited	• Willemite
Faith	• Malachite • Pipestone
Femininity	• Chrysocolla • Moonstone
Fidelity	• Agate • Malachite
Firm	• Pink Angel Wing Dolomite
Flexible	• Anhydrite
Flowing, Flow With	• Peridot • Pharmocosiderite • Sodalite • Zoisite

≈≈≈≈≈≈≈≈≈≈≈≈≈≈≈≈

Energy State	**Crystals**
Fortunate	• Adamite • Apache Tear • Cat's Eye • Regency Rose Agate
Free	• Amethyst • Calcite • Silver
Friendship	• Iris Agate
Fulfilled	• Bloodstone • Ceruleite • Sapphire
Genuine	• Serpentine
Good Natured	• Phillipsburgite
Graced	• Royal Plume Jasper
Graceful	• Serpentine
Grounded	• Black Agate • Rhyolite
Happy	• Hermatite • Iris Agate • Regency Rose Agate • Sardonyx
Harmonious	• Altaite
Healing Energy	• Rosasite
Heartwholeness	• Adamite • Ajoite • Obsidian • Rose Quartz • Sodalite • Sugilite
Honesty	• Red Jasper

≈≈≈≈≈≈≈≈≈≈≈≈≈≈≈≈

Energy State	**Crystals**
Honorable	• Tin
Humble	• Pyrope
Idea Generating	• Fluorite • Plume Agate • Topaz
Imaginative	• Amazonite
Impartial	• Ajoite
Independent	• Petoskey Stone
Industrious	• Fire Opal
Inner Awareness	• Amethyst • Blue Lace Agate • Chrysoprase • Hematite • Sphene
Insightful	• Chrysoprase • Purple Sage Agate • Tourmaline
Inspired	• Bloodstone • Topaz
Integrity	• Topaz
Intellectual	• Altaite • Laguna Agate
Intelligent	• Pyrite
Interrelated	• Lepidocrocite
Introspective	• Chrysoprase • Purple Sage Agate
Intuitive	• Antigorite

≈≈≈≈≈≈≈≈≈≈≈≈≈≈≈≈≈

Energy State	Crystals
Invigorated	• Copper • Mica • Uranophane
Involved	• Ussingite
Joyful	• Chalcedony • Citrine • Lavender Quartz • Sardonyx • Snakeskin Agate
Kundalini Movement	• Angel Wing Agate
Leadership	• Iolite
Liberated	• Phenacite • Silver
Life Growth	• Cerussite
Living in Present	• Bloodstone
Longevity	• Turquoise
Lovable	• Andean Opal • Moss Agate • Pearl • Rhodochrosite
Love	• Almandine • Aquamarine • Beryl, Carnelian • Emerald • Moss Agate • Mother of Pearl • Pearl • Rose Quartz • Sugilite

≈≈≈≈≈≈≈≈≈≈≈≈≈≈≈≈

Energy State	**Crystals**
Loyal	• Malachite
Male/Female Balance	• Rhodonite • Rose-eye Agate • Tiger Eye
Manifestation	• Adamite • Amber
Masculinity	• Tourmaline
Mature	• Sapphire
Meditation	• Chrysoprase • Dry-head Agate • Iolite
Mellow	• Ajoite • Corundum • Smoky Quartz
Motivated	• Barite • Tiger Eye
Open	• Pyrite
Open to Truth	• Ajoite • Bornite • Chrysoprase
Open-minded	• Blue Opal
Orderly	• Diamond
Organized	• Diamond • Flint
Outgoing	• Gibbsite • Polka Dot Agate
Pampered	• Rutilated Topaz
Passion	• Rhodochrosite

≈≈≈≈≈≈≈≈≈≈≈≈≈≈≈≈

Energy State	Crystals
Past Life Recall	• Amber • Carnelian
Patience	• Dry-head Agate • Pearl
Peace	• Ajoite • Alexandrite • Amazonite • Aquamarine • Calcite • Kunzite • Pearl • Sardonyx • Zircon
Performance	• Adularia • Fire Agate
Perspective	• Alurgite • Iolite • Lavender Quartz
Persuasive	• Carnalite
Positive Mind-set	• Gold
Power	• Rutilated Topaz
Productive	• Adularia • Brown Zircon
Prosperous	• Adamite • Cat's Eye • Sapphire

≈≈≈≈≈≈≈≈≈≈≈≈≈≈≈≈≈

Energy State	Crystals
Protected	• Acanthite • Aegirine • Apache Tear • Cat's Eye • Chalcedony • Snowflake Obsidian • Turquoise
Pure	• Pearl • Silver
Purposeful	• White Onyx
Receptivity	• Chalcedony
Relationship Enhancing	• Beryl
Relaxed	• Ammonite • Lapis Lazuli • Onyx • Smoky Quartz • Zircon
Released	• Pipestone • Uranophane
Reliable	• Yellow Zircon
Rejoiceful	• Citrine • Scorodite
Rejuvenated	• Diaspor • Selenite
Relieved	• Pumice
Resolute	• Pumice • Reddingite
Responsible	• Pyrope

≈≈≈≈≈≈≈≈≈≈≈≈≈≈≈≈

Energy State	Crystals
Restored	• Diaspor • Serpentine
Revitalized	• Copper • Pink Angel Wing Dolomite
Romance	• Moonstone
Safe	• Acanthite • Chalcedony • Turquoise
Satisfied	• Uranophane
Self-acceptance	• Aegirine • Ajoite
Self-assurance	• Agate • Chrysocolla
Self-confident	• Apache Tear • Chrysocolla • Pumice • Snakeskin Agate
Self-esteem	• Aegirine • Alexandrite • Snakeskin Agate
Self-reliant	• Petalite • Selenite
Self-sufficient	• Stilbite
Sensitive Psychically	• Goethite • Purple Sage Agate
Serene	• Aquamarine • Dioptase • Ivory • Sardonyx • Zircon

≈≈≈≈≈≈≈≈≈≈≈≈≈≈≈≈≈

Energy State	**Crystals**
Sharing	• Petarasite
Sincere	• Obsidian • Plattnerite
Skillful	• Kornerupine
Solution-oriented	• Botswana Agate • Citrine • Pumice
Soothing	• Amber • Amblygonite • Onyx
Spiritually Aware	• Adularia • Amethyst
Spiritual Sexuality	• Black Opal • Garnet
Spontaneous	• Green Tourmaline
Stabile	• Ammonite • Dioptase • Emerald
Strong	• Agate • Brazilian Agate
Subconscious Thoughts	• Jasper
Success	• Apache Tear • Fire Agate • Tiger Eye • Turritella Agate
Supported	• Peridot
Sustained	• Sellaite
Tactful	• Albite

≈≈≈≈≈≈≈≈≈≈≈≈≈≈≈≈

Energy State	Crystals
Telepathic	• Amethyst • Angle Wing Agate • Apache Tear • Beryl
Tenacious	• Brazilian Agate • Petrified Wood
Tender	• Touchstone
Tolerant	• Aquamarine • Moss Agate
Tranquil	• Amazonite • Calcite • Green Jade • Kunzite • Phenacite • Ruby
Transformation	• Diaspor • Peridot • Pipestone
Transitions (Easy)	• Lepidolite • Peridot • Riverstone
Trust	• Lodestone
Trustworthy	• Diamond
Truth	• Aquamarine • Purple Sage Agate
Unconditional Love	• Millerite • Moss Agate • Pearl

≈≈≈≈≈≈≈≈≈≈≈≈≈≈≈≈

Energy State	Crystals
Understanding	• Adamite • Chrysocolla • Plume Agate • Purple Sage Agate
Unified	• Ambligonite • Clear Quartz • Tiger Eye
Unrestrained	• Chert
Uplifted	• Citrine • Emerald
Vibrant	• Petoskey Stone
Valued	• Platinum
Victorious	• Copal
Virile	• Sellaite
Virtuous	• Sheet Topaz
Visionary	• Iolite • Tourmaline
Vital	• Green Topaz • Honey Zircon
Vitality	• Copper
Youthful	• Chrysoprase
Warm	• Erythrite
Willpower	• Apache Tear
Wise	• Pumice
Worthy	• Alexandrite • Willemite
Yielding	• Anhydrite • Trona

≈≈≈≈≈≈≈≈≈≈≈≈≈≈≈≈≈

CHAPTER 6

USING A PENDULUM TO FIND THE OPTIMAL CRYSTAL

Definition of Dowsing

Dowsing is the ancient art of detecting objects that have a natural electromagnetic field. Water divining, or the ability to locate a water source under the surface of the Earth, is probably the oldest known form of dowsing. The tools for dowsing have traditionally been a Y rod, the L rods, or a pendulum. When dowsing for the optimal crystal, you will learn how to use a pendulum.

Today, many mineral and mining companies, water companies, and farmers employ dowsers on their payroll. Such people would not use dowsers unless dowsing worked. When our neighbors had a block in their water line, the water company sent a dowser to determine the location of the blockage. They did not want to disturb the entire yard looking for the blockage when they could limit the extent of their digging. Dowsing is also used frequently by alternative health practitioners due to the ability of dowsing to diagnose physiological and biochemical deficiencies at a level much subtler than traditional laboratory tests.

How Dowsing Works

Dowsing is essentially communication that is based on electromagnetic energy. Everything has an electromagnetic field -- animate physical beings like a human being or a dog or a bird, inanimate physical beings like water or the Earth, and intangible energy like your superconscious awareness or Spirit. The electromagnetic field creates a flow of energy that can move physical objects like pendulums when that intent is programmed. When you program a swinging pendulum to react in certain ways to certain conditions, the pendulum will respond that way every time.

The real detector in dowsing is the dowser, i.e., the electromagnetic field working with the subconscious mind. The dowser is actually programming his or her subconscious mind rather than the pendulum. The subconscious is in charge of the automatic body functions like breathing and pulse rate. Because it runs the body, the subconscious has the ability to create movement such as swinging a pendulum. The dowsing instrument is simply like the needle on a meter. It indicates what is unconsciously already known as it taps into the universal knowledge of the collective unconscious. Therefore, it is necessary for a dowser to be very clear about what they wish to detect. Learning to maintain the correct attitude and clarity of intention is critical to dowsing correctly. If the dowser is emotionally upset, the disturbances in the electromagnetic field can affect the dowsing instrument which would result in an inaccurate reading. Some of the factors that can adversely affect dowsing include preconceived opinions about the answer, fear regarding the ability to dowse, doubt about the dowsing process, or mental fatigue.

Because the subconscious controls automatic body functions such as heart rate, pulse, breathing, blinking, involuntary muscle response, and so forth, one can train it to take direction and move a dowsing mechanism in the direction of "yes" or "no" in response to questions. Once the subconscious is trained vis-à-vis the dowsing mechanism which direction is "yes" and which is "no", it will swing in response to incoming electromagnetic energy. For those who wish to work with spiritual counsel but feel telepathically blocked, the dowsing instrument is a good way to receive input to questions via electromagnetic energy.

≈≈≈≈≈≈≈≈≈≈≈≈≈≈≈≈

The subconscious holds the ability to be in touch with the non-physical world of Spirit which holds a vast array of information beyond our physical awareness level. However, we have difficulty moving the subconscious information into our conscious or mental state, primarily due to interference from our own judgment. We may receive strong intuitive hunches, but our logical side might dismiss them. Or, our rational side explains away anything that is not conceivable through our five senses. A pendulum bypasses logic or judgment and taps into what cannot be seen or heard. It is an excellent tool for bridging the gap between physical and non-physical, conscious and subconscious. The dowsing instrument is nothing more than a way to bypass the myriad of preconceived notions that are generated by the conscious mind. The conscious mind formulates a question and presents it to the subconscious. The subconscious mind gets the "unedited" answer from the superconscious.

Muscle testing or kinesiology is used by many chiropractors to obtain information on skeletal misalignment. The subconscious is in charge of managing body functions. It is accustomed to running the body without direction from the conscious. It can be programmed to cause muscles to be strong for a true statement and weak for a false statement or condition. Some chiropractors ask patients to lay face down, and they work with the patient's feet, asking questions about skeletal alignment and looking for a strong or weak response as they push against the feet. Other chiropractors have patients extend an arm away from the body and resist against a downward touch, once again, checking for a strong or weak muscle response as they touch various structural elements in the body. If the patient needs an adjustment, the muscles are weak and the subconscious cannot resist against the pressure. They are in a weakened state. If the skeletal structure is aligned, the muscles are strong and the subconscious can easily resist the pressure.

The Dowsing Instrument

A pendulum can be used to select crystals for broadcasting. Pendulums come in all shapes and sizes, and they can be purchased at metaphysical bookstores or through the Internet. InterLink also stocks pendulums at www.annebrewer.com.

One word of caution about selecting a pendulum. It is best NOT to use a pendulum with a crystal on it. Naturally, people like them because they are pretty and seem more spiritual. However, a crystal can transmit and receive energy signals. That is why they are used in radios and for crystal broadcasting. They are transmitting devices! When an object is used for transmitting and receiving energy as well as for measuring electromagnetic responses to questions through the subconscious, one risks receiving muddled information. The crystal might absorb energy which affects the reading. Needless to say, one circumvents the likelihood of receiving misinformation from a pendulum by using one made of wood, plastic, stone, glass, or a metal like brass or copper.

The Dowsing Position

When holding a pendulum, dangle it from at least a three inch length of string or chain. That way, you can feel differences in intensity when the pendulum swings. For example, a strong "yes" will swing back and forth with great gusto while a weak "yes" will wobble weakly back and forth. Do not hold your arm against your body as this tends to dampen the response.

Here are several suggestions for eliminating your influence on the sway of the pendulum:

≈≈≈≈≈≈≈≈≈≈≈≈≈≈≈≈

- If you want to convince your conscious mind that you are not physically involved in moving the pendulum, do not hold the actual chain. Hold the pendulum by a loop or O-ring at the top of the string or chain between your thumb and forefinger, palm facing downward. That way, the pendulum cannot be nudged into action by you.
- After grasping the loop or O-ring, place your elbow on a flat surface (e.g., a table) and raise your arm at a 45 degree angle to the table, allowing the pendulum to swing freely from your grasp. When you place your elbow on a stationery surface, you are less likely to be able to physically influence the movement of the pendulum. After you gain more confidence in your dowsing ability, you will find that you do not need to position your elbow.

Programming A Pendulum

Your subconscious must be programmed to swing the pendulum in a specific direction for a specific answer, either "yes", "no", or "maybe". You need a mutual set of commands from which both you and your pendulum are operating. A pendulum will use the energy of your electromagnetic field to swing the mechanism. But it must have a repertoire of signals for communication purposes, or it would be like using Morse code without the code book.

There are a multitude of ways to program a pendulum. Some prefer a clockwise circle to indicate "yes" and a counterclockwise circle to indicate "no". Some use a piece of paper that has numbers and percentages on it, and they swing their pendulum over the paper, training it to "read" the symbols, much like a Ouija board utilizes the alphanumeric characters to provide information. Some train the pendulum to swing toward the body and away from the body ("north/south") for "yes" and parallel to the body ("east/west") for "no". The pendulum hovers in the middle in a small clockwise circle for maybe. This is faster than the clockwise/counterclockwise method because the pendulum can shift back and forth very quickly between "yes" and "no". It does not need to come to a complete stop in order to reverse direction. You need to decide which method works best for you and program your pendulum to use it.

To program your subconscious, hold the pendulum by the chain or string and tell your subconscious that you are going to show it how to indicate a "yes" on the pendulum. Force the pendulum to swing in the "north/south" direction or whatever you have designated for yes." You can even tell your subconscious, "This is like shaking our head "yes". Repeat this intentional swing for "no" and "maybe". You may want to repeat the intentional swings several times each for "yes", "no", and "maybe" to ensure that your subconscious receives the information accurately.

Next, test your programming by asking a question for which you have the answer. For example, if you are 35 years old, ask "Am I currently 35 years old?" Again, nudge your pendulum into a "yes" swing in order to assist it. Then ask, "Am I currently 40 years old?" Nudge, your pendulum into a "no" position. Although I say you are training your pendulum, you are really training your subconscious which manages involuntary body functions like the electromagnetic field to work with the pendulum. This pendulum, and any other pendulum used, is now ready to respond with answers on an electromagnetic level. Some people are particular about using a specific pendulum or not allowing other people to use their pendulum. Remember, the subconscious is being programmed, not the pendulum!

After you have helped your pendulum understand "yes", "no", and whatever other indicators you desire, you are ready to hold the pendulum and ask questions without assisting it. Grasp the pendulum by the loop at the top of the chain. Ask simple questions to which you know the answers until your pendulum responds involuntarily. This should be relatively simple to accomplish. However, it takes some people longer than others. You will encounter easy success if you do not over-think this process. Everyone has electromagnetic energy. Therefore, everyone can easily make a pendulum work for them.

Robert Detzler, author of *Soul Re-Creation*, a book describing a healing process that requires a pendulum, has addressed what to do when a pendulum does not work. Sometimes there are actual blocks that need to be removed in order to be able to dowse. Perhaps a new dowser has never before attempted telepathic contact with Spirit, and there are soul memories of prior lifetimes of being punished for obtaining psychic information. Or maybe one has been raised to follow strict religious doctrines that do not recognize psychism. The subconscious may feel fear and shut down. Or it may simply mean the conscious mind does not believe in the ability to use a pendulum. This is what Robert Detzler recommends to clear dowsing blocks:

Speak one or more of the following clearing statements out loud.

- I release all fear of using the pendulum.
- I release all belief, perception, and judgment that I cannot or should not use a pendulum.
- I release all need and desire to believe that I cannot or should not use a pendulum.
- I now completely accept and believe on every level of my conscious and subconscious being that I will receive strong signals and accurate information.

In the beginning, you may find it necessary to use the releasing statements several times to obtain cooperation from the subconscious mind.

≈≈≈≈≈≈≈≈≈≈≈≈≈≈≈≈

The Questions

Your pendulum answers are only as accurate as your questions. You must be very specific and clear, or you will obtain erroneous results. For example, you might have misplaced the car keys so you try to narrow down the location by asking "Are my keys in the house"? The pendulum swings "yes", so you spend an hour searching for car keys, finally giving up in vain after locating two sets of spare house keys and some luggage keys. Eventually, you find the car keys in the driveway. The pendulum was correct. Your HOUSE and LUGGAGE keys were in the house. However, your CAR keys were not. Asking accurate questions is the most difficult part of dowsing. Be as specific as possible. Your subconscious is VERY literal.

A good rule of thumb is to only ask questions about information that exists somewhere. Do not ask for an opinion when there are no agreed-upon reference points, and there is too much room for interpretation. When using a pendulum for crystal broadcasting, you will ask a question, then hold the pendulum over pre-determined answers on the charts. Or, you will say specific names of crystals aloud. This will minimize any erroneous answers.

Permission and Accuracy

Sometimes you do not have permission to obtain information. Perhaps you are asking for information, and it is not spiritually correct for you to have that information. Or you may be asking for future information which would affect decisions you need to make without knowledge of the future. Please note that future is very difficult to dowse accurately among the best of the dowsers. This is due to the fact that we have free choice and free will, and our future is not set in stone. It is always best when dowsing to focus on now rather than future, which will not be a problem when dowsing for the best crystal to use.

≈≈≈≈≈≈≈≈≈≈≈≈≈≈≈≈

However, in crystal broadcasting you will need to dowse how long to keep the crystal on your resolution sheet. It is always best to re-dowse the question at the end of the predicted time period. You may have encountered situations during the broadcasting process that caused resistance, thereby extending the anticipated time.

Your subconscious will only override an accurate answer to a question when you are emotionally vested in the outcome. It should not cause you problems when dowsing for a crystal for broadcasting since you are not emotionally vested in which crystal to use. It is always easier to dowse accurately for others, especially when you are not emotionally involved, because your subconscious does not have an agenda.

When asking questions of non-physical beings in the spiritual world, be sure to specify that you wish to speak to your high self. All of us have a high self or Godself which holds superconscious knowledge. This superconscious knowing is retrievable via the subconscious because it is connected by an energy cord to the high self. Access information, even crystals for broadcasting, through the high self, then, you know exactly who is providing the information. There are plenty of disembodied souls or discarnates. If you do not specify who you are calling, anyone could pick up the receiver on the other end.

To circumvent inaccuracies, always dowse the answers to the following series of questions prior to asking your main question. If you do not receive a "yes" to each of the following questions, then do not proceed with your dowsing.

- Do I have permission from the Divine Creator/God/Source to ask this question?
- Am I working with my high self?
- Am I able to receive 100% accurate information on my question concerning (situation) today?

≈≈≈≈≈≈≈≈≈≈≈≈≈≈≈≈

If you obtain a “no” to the second question, you might want to drop down to 95%, 90%, and so forth, to see how accurate you can be. You may be able to live with a 90% accuracy rate for your question. You can also ask your high self to clear any blocks or barriers that are interfering with your ability to receive accurate information. If you repeat the same questions and still receive a “no”, then either ask someone else to dowse for you or use the tables in this book to identify the optimal crystal.

The best way to learn how to dowse is to practice. Practice receiving answers and living the results to determine your level of accuracy.

≈≈≈≈≈≈≈≈≈≈≈≈≈≈≈≈

CHAPTER 7

DOWSING FOR THE OPTIMAL CRYSTAL

Rationale for Dowsing

Based on researching which crystals to use for my own clearing, I discovered it is not always possible to determine the best crystal by reading the metaphysical books that define the characteristics of each crystal. Sometimes the conditions you wish to clear are very specific, and you cannot locate that particular condition. Sometimes the interpretations of the authors of these books are broad, and you can easily misinterpret which crystal holds the optimal molecular structure to address your issue. Although there are lists that identify which crystal to use, you are well-served to practice dowsing to identify the crystal that works best for you, whether you are confirming the best crystal that is already listed on the charts or starting from scratch on the crystal lists.

At this point, you have read the section on how to dowse with a pendulum and are aware of the dowsing process. The following lists of minerals and gemstones have been developed by researching both metaphysical and geological references. You can dowse with the pendulum to identify which crystal to use.

Notice that the lists are comprised of names that are either in regular or bold type. It is difficult to locate some crystals. Therefore the **bold** type identifies the items I have been able to locate, either in rock shops, at gem and mineral shows, in catalogs, or over the Internet. This way you will know which items are relatively easy to find and which ones may be more challenging.

There is a limited directory of crystal sources in the appendix. If you are an Internet user, you can visit some of the websites and see which ones work best for you. There are hundreds of listings for mineral and gemstone sources. You will find that you can link endlessly from one website to another, once you are in these websites. After you determine the site you wish to use, you can e-mail your request for a particular item if it is not listed. Be sure to explain that you do not need large pieces or high quality specimens since many of these sites sell to collectors for display. Some of the sites in the appendix are internationally located. They tend to carry some of the more unusual specimens and accept major credit cards. Remember, be practical. There is no need to spend a lot of money on a perfect or large specimen.

If you do not have Internet access, you can use the phone numbers in the appendix to contact the various suppliers. Some of them offer catalogs free-of-charge or for a nominal fee if you wish to keep a list on hand for reference. You might also wish to purchase a *Lapidary Journal* since it lists the various gem and mineral show schedules and locations across the country as well as a plethora of retail sources.

How to Use the Alphabetical Charts

Review the crystal chart format on the following pages prior to reading these instructions. The instructions will make more sense after you have seen the format. All of the items are listed alphabetically. Items are not grouped by category. In other words, there may be several types of garnets, but each is listed individually and alphabetically under their particular name. When an item is part of a larger grouping, the larger grouping is identified. For example, moss agate is listed under "M", but it is a form of chalcedony, as indicated in parentheses. You may be able to use either moss agate, which is very specific, or any type of chalcedony. Again, you can dowse to determine if both the item and the group are equally beneficial for broadcasting. In addition to indicating the family or group for specific crystals, the groups are listed in alphabetical order. If you initially dowse the entire group, this means you can probably use any item that falls within that particular category.

Although tedious, it is best if you read the names of the items on each chart. You do not need to consciously memorize the charts. But your subconscious memory should "know" which crystals are listed, or your subconscious has no record of the possible outcomes when dowsing. When you read the list, it is like entering the data in your database so it can easily be retrieved during the dowsing process.

The following series of questions are suggestions that can be employed when dowsing for the optimal crystal. Naturally, you can create your own questions.

1. Begin by checking on your source and level of accuracy (see page 88).

2. State: "I am dowsing to determine the optimal crystal from the alphabetical lists for the purposes of clearing (CONDITIONS LISTED IN "NEW CONDITION" COLUMN ON RESOLUTION SHEET)."

3. You may want to determine, "Is there more than one item listed that will effectively model and broadcast the conditions I desire?" Determine the correct number of items.

4. If you have multiple possibilities, dowse for them one at a time. Ask, "Does my item appear on the "A" through "M" list?" If you receive a "yes", then narrow it down to the "A" through "F" list, or the "G" through "M" list. Determine the correct beginning letter by dowsing, "Is it "A"?, "Is it "B"? etc. until you obtain a "yes" on your pendulum.

5. After determining which alphabetical list you should use, ask, "Does the name of my item

appear in Column "A"? If "no", continue with Column "B" and "C" until you have located the correct column.

6. To further narrow the possibilities, you can ask if the name of your item is listed in bold type. If it is, then you need only check the bold listings. If it is not, you only need to check the non-bold names. You can also reduce the names you need to dowse by asking if the item is in the top half or bottom half of the column. You can use your finger to point to the name, asking, "Is it this one?", without stating the name aloud. If you receive a "no", continue with the next name.

7. Some crystals are available in a wide variety of colors. The color of the crystal may or may not be important. Determine the importance of color by asking, "Do I need to use a specific color of (CRYSTAL) to model my (NEW CONDITIONS)?" If you receive a "yes", you can either refer to a rock and mineral book to determine which colors are available and dowse for the correct color, or you can wait until you view the specimens on the Internet or in a rock shop and dowse for the correct color at that time.

8. Once you have obtained the item or items that are capable of modeling and broadcasting the conditions you wish to achieve on your Resolution Sheet, verify your results by asking, "I have identified (CRYSTAL) to model and broadcast my (CONDITIONS LISTED ON "NEW CONDITION" COLUMN OF RESOLUTION SHEET). Is this correct?" If you receive a "yes", continue. If you receive a "no", return to the charts.

9. Now that you have identified the crystal required to broadcast your desired condition, you will need to procure it. Visit your local rock or mineral shop or contact one of the sources in the appendix.

≈≈≈≈≈≈≈≈≈≈≈≈≈≈≈≈

You may also wish to purchase one of the new age crystal interpretation books that lists the various crystals and their corresponding properties. Two popular books are Melody's *Love is in the Earth, A Kaleidoscope of Crystals* or Judithann H. David's and JP Van Hulle's *Michael's Gemstone Dictionary*.

≈≈≈≈≈≈≈≈≈≈≈≈≈≈≈≈

≈≈≈≈≈≈≈≈≈≈≈≈≈≈≈≈

ALPHABETICAL CHARTS

≈≈≈≈≈≈≈≈≈≈≈≈≈≈≈≈≈

A's: Column A	A's: Column B	A's: Column C
Abalone	**Amethyst (Quartz)**	**Apatite**
Acanthite	**Ametrine**	Aphrizite
Acmite	Amianthus (Actinolite)	**Apophyllite**
Actinolite	**Ammonite**	**Aquamarine (Beryl)**
Adamite	**Amphibole (Group)**	**Aragonite (Group)**
Adelite (Group)	**Analcite**	**Ardennite**
Adularia (Orthoclase)	**Anapaite**	**Arfvedsonite (Amphibole)**
Aegirine (Pyroxene)	**Anatase**	**Argentite**
Aeschynite	Ancroite (Tourmaline)	Arizona Lizard Jasper
Agalmatolite (Talc)	**Andalusite**	**Arrojadite**
Agardite (Mixite)	Andean Opal	**Arsenic (Group)**
Agate (Quartz)	Andesine (Feldspar)	**Arseniosiderite**
Agrinierite	**Andersonite**	Arsenoclasite
Aheylite (Turquoise)	**Andradite (Garnet)**	**Arsenopyrite (Group)**
Ajoite	Andrewsite	**Arsenotsunbite**
Akatoreite	Angel Wing Agate	Arsenuranylite
Alabandite	**Anglesite (Barite)**	**Arthurite (Group)**
Alabaster	**Anhydrite**	**Artinite**
Albite (Feldspar)	**Ankerite (Dolomite)**	Asbolite (Linnaeite)
Alexandrite (Chrysoberyl)	**Annabergite (Vivianite)**	**Astrophyllite (Group)**
Alforsite (Apatite)	Anorthite (Feldspar)	**Atacamite**
Almandine (Garnet)	**Anthophyllite (Amphibole)**	Atelestite
Allanite (Epidote)	Antigorite (Serpentine)	**Augelite**
Alunite (Group)	**Antimonite (Antimony)**	**Augite (Pyroxene)**
Alurgite	**Antimony (Arsenic)**	**Aurichalcite**
Amalcime	**Antlerite**	**Australian Opal**
Amakinite (Brucite)	Anyolite (Zoisite)	**Autunite (Group)**
Amazonite (Microcline)	**Apache Tear (Obsidian)**	**Aventurine (Quartz)**
Amber		Avogadrite
Amblygonite (Group)		**Axinite**
		Azulicite
		Azurite

≈≈≈≈≈≈≈≈≈≈≈≈≈≈≈≈≈

B's: Column A	B's: Column B	B's: Column C
Banded Agate	**Bertrandite**	Botryogen
Bauxite	**Beryl**	**Boulangerite**
Babingtonite	Beryllonite	**Boulder Opal**
Baculites	Berzeliite	**Bournonite**
Bahianite	Beta Quartz	Bowenite
Bakerite (Gadolinite)	**Betafite**	Brachelbuschite (Group)
Balameroite	Beudantite (Group)	Brandtite
Baratovite	Bieberite	**Braunite**
Barbetonite (Manasseite)	**Binitoite**	Bravoite
Barite (Group)	**Biotite**	**Brazilian Agate**
Barroisite	**Bismuth (Group)**	**Brazilianite**
Barysilite	**Bismuthinite**	Brecciated Agate
Barytocalcite	**Bityite**	**Brewsterite (Zeolite)**
Basalt	**Bixbyite**	**Brochantite**
Basinite	Bjarebyite (Group	**Bronzite**
Bat Cave Jasper	Bloedite	**Brookite**
Bauxite	**Bloodstone (Hematite)**	Brown Spar (Ankerite)
Bavenite	**Boji Stones**	Bruneau Jasper
Beaverite	**Boleite**	**Brucite (Group)**
Benitoite	Bolivarite	**Brushite**
Benjaninite	Boothite	Buergerite (Tourmaline)
Berguerite	**Boracite**	Bunsenite
Berlinite	Borate (Group)	Bustamite
Berthierite	Borax	Butlerite
	Bornite	**Bytownite (Feldspar)**

≈≈≈≈≈≈≈≈≈≈≈≈≈≈≈≈

C's: Column A	C's: Column B	C's: Column C
Cacoxenite	Chamosite	**Conichalcite**
Cafarsite	**Charoite**	**Connellite**
Cahnite	**Chenevixite**	Connemara
Calaverite	Cheralite IMonazite)	**Cookeite (Chlorite)**
Calcite (Group)	**Cherry Opal**	**Copal**
Caledonite	**Chert**	Copiapite (Group)
Calomel	**Chiastolite (Andalusite)**	**Copper**
Cancrinite (Group)	**Childrenite**	**Coprolite**
Cappelenite	Chloanthite	Coquimbite
Carletonite	**Chlorargyrite**	**Coral**
Carminite	**Chlorite (Group)**	**Cordierite**
Carnallite	Chloritoid	Corkite (Beudantite)
Carnelian	Chlorocalcite	**Cornetite**
Carnigorm	Chloromelanite (Jadeite)	**Corundum (Hematite)**
Carnotite	Chloroxiphite	**Covellite**
Carrollite (Linnaeite)	**Chondrodite (Humite)**	**Coyamite Agate**
Cassiterite (Rutile)	**Chromite**	Cowrie
Catlinite	**Chrysanthemum Stn.**	Crazy Lace Agate
Cat's Eye (Chrysoberyl)	**Chrysoberyl**	**Creedite**
Cat's Eye (Quartz)	**Chrysocolla**	**Cristobalite (Quartz)**
Cat's Eye (Tourmaline)	**Chrysoprase**	**Crococite**
Cavansite	**Chrysotile**	**Crocoite (Riebeckite)**
Celadonite (Mica)	Chudobaite	Crossite
Celestine (Barite)	**Churchite**	**Cryolite**
Celestite	**Cinnabar**	Cryptomelane (Group)
Ceruleite	**Citrine (Quartz)**	**Cubanite**
Cerussite (Aragonite)	**Clear Quartz**	Cumberlandite
Chabazite (Zeolite)	**Cleavelandite**	Cummingtonite (Amphibole)
Chalcanthite (Group)	**Clinochlore (Chlorite)**	**Cuprite**
Chalcedony	**Clinoclase**	**Cuproadamite**
Chalcocite	**Clinoptilolite (Zeolite)**	Cuprolite
Chalcopyrite (Group)	**Clinozoisite (Epidote)**	**Cuprosklodowskite**
Chalcotrichite (Cuprite)	**Coal**	**Cuspidine**
Chalcosiderite (Turquoise)	**Cobaltite (Group)**	**Cyanotrichite**
Chapmanite	**Colemanite**	**Cylindrite**
	Columbite	Cymophane
	Condor Agate	**Cymrite**

≈≈≈≈≈≈≈≈≈≈≈≈≈≈≈≈≈

D's: Column A	D's: Column B	D's: Column C
Damsonite	**Desert Rose Gypsum**	**Dolomite (Rock)**
Danalite	**Devilline**	Donathite
Danburite	Diabantite	Domeykite
Daphnite	**Diadochite**	Douglasite
Darwin Glass	**Diamond**	**Dravite (Tourmaline)**
Datolite (Gadolinite)	Diaspore	**Drusy Quartz**
Davyne	Dicinite	Dry Head Agate
Dechenite	**Dickite (Kaolinite-Serpentine)**	**Duftite (Adelite)**
Demantoid (Anhydrite)	**Dinosaur Bone**	Dumontite
Dendritic Opal	**Diopside (Pyroxene)**	**Dumortierite**
Dendritic Quartz	**Dioptase**	**Dundasite**
Desautelsite (Hydrotalcite)	**Dogtooth Calcite**	Dypingite
Descloizite (Group)	**Dolomite (Group)**	**Dyscrasite**

E's: Column A	E's: Column B	E's: Column C
Ecdemne	Emmonsite	**Erionite (Zeolite)**
Eckermannite (Amphibole)	Empressite	**Erythrite (Vivianite)**
Edenite (Amphibole)	**Enargite**	Erythrosiderite
Edingtonite (Zeolite)	**Endlichite**	**Esperite**
Eglestonite	Enhydros Agate	**Ettringite (Group)**
Eilat	**Enstatite (Pyroxene)**	Euchroite
Elbaite (Tourmaline)	**Eosphorite**	**Euclase**
Elephant Ear Coral	**Epididymite**	**Eudialyte**
Embolite	**Epidote (Group)**	Eulite
Emerald (Beryl)	**Epistilbite (Zeolite)**	**Evansite**
	Epsomite	Eveite

F's: Column A	F's: Column B	F's: Column C
Fassaite (Pyrocene)	Fiedlerite	**Fluorite**
Faujasite (Zeolite)	Fillowite	**Fluorspar**
Faustite (Turquoise)	**Fire Agate**	**Fluororichterite (Amphibole)**
Fayalite (Olivine)	**Fire Opal**	**Foid (Group)**
Feldspar (Group)	**Fire Quartz**	**Forsterite (Olivine)**
Feldspathoids (Group)	Flame Agate	Fourmarierite
Fenster Quartz	**Flint**	**Franckeite**
Ferberite (Fluorite)	**Fluorapatite (Apatite)**	**Franklinite (Spinel)**
Fergusonite	Florencite (Crandallite)	**Freibergite (Tetrahedrite)**
Fernandinite	**Fluellite**	**Fuchsite**
Ferrierite (Zeolite)	**Fluorescence**	**Fulgurite**
Ferro-axinite (Axinite)	**Fluororichterite (Amphibole)**	
Fersmanite		

≈≈≈≈≈≈≈≈≈≈≈≈≈≈≈≈≈

G's: Column A	G's: Column B	G's: Column C
Gadolinite (Group)	Glaucodot (Arsenopyrite)	Grandidierite
Galena	**Glauconite (Mica)**	**Granite**
Ganophyllite	Glaucophane (Amphibole)	**Graphite**
Garnet (Group)	**Gmelinite (Zeolite)**	Gratonite
Gaudefroyite	**Gneiss**	**Gray Lace Agate**
Gehlenite (Melilite)	**Goethite**	**Greenockite**
Genthelvite	**Gold**	**Green Tree Jasper**
Geode	**Gorceixite (Crandallite)**	**Grolite**
Gibbsite	Goshenite (Beryl)	**Grossularite Garnet**
Girasol	**Goudeyite (Mixite)**	**Guerinite**
Gismondine (Zeolite)	Goyazite (Crandallite)	**Guinea Jasper**
Glass (Natural)		**Gypsum**
Glauberite		**Gyrolite**

H's: Column A	H's: Column B	H's: Column C
Halite	Hendricksite (Mica)	**Hopeite**
Halotrichite (Group)	**Herderite (Gadolinite)**	**Hornblende**
Hambergite	**Herkimer Diamond**	Hornesite (Vivianite)
Hanksite	Herrerite	**Howlite**
Harkerite	**Hessonite (Garnet)**	**Hubnerite**
Harlequin Quartz	Heterosite	**Huelandite**
Harmotome (Zeolite)	**Heulandite (Zeolite)**	**Humite (Group)**
Hauerite (Pyrite)	**Hewettite**	Hummerite
Hausmannite	Hexagonite	**Huntite**
Hauyne (Sodalite)	**Hiddenite (Spodumene)**	**Hureaulite**
Heazlewoodite	Hodgkinsonite	Hyalophane (Feldspar)
Hedenbergite (Pyrocene)	Holdenite	Hydrargillite
Heinrichite (Autunite)	Hollandite (Cryptomelane)	Hydrogrossularite (Garnet)
Heliodor (Beryl)	Holly Agate	Hydromagnesite
Heliotrope	**Holley**	Hydrotalcite (Group)
Hematite (Group)	**Holtite**	Hydrozincite
Hemimorphite	**Homilite (Gadolinite)**	Hypersthene

I's: Column A	I's: Column B	I's: Column C
Iceland Spar Calcite	Imperial Topaz	Iridosmine
Idocrase	**Indicolite (Pyrocene)**	Iris Agate
Ilmenite (Group)	**Inesite**	**Iron**
Ilvaite	**Iolite**	**Ivory**
Imperial Jasper	Iridarsenite	

≈≈≈≈≈≈≈≈≈≈≈≈≈≈≈≈≈

J's: Column A	J's: Column B	J's: Column C
Jade/Jadeite (Pyroxene)	**Jasper (Chalcedony)**	**Joaquinite (Group)**
Jahnsite	Jelly Opal	Johannsenite
Jamesonite	Jeremejevite	Jokokuite (Chalcanthite)
Jarosite (Alunite)	**Jet**	Julienite
	Jinshajiangite	

K's: Column A	K's: Column B	K's: Column C
Kaemmererite (Chlorite)	**Kempite**	Koksharovite
Kainite	**Kernite**	**Kolbeckite**
Kainosite	Kettnerite	Kolwezite (Rosasite)
Kaliophilite	**Kidwellite**	**Kornerupine**
Kaolinite (Group)	Kieserite (Group)	**Kulanite (Bjarebyite)**
Kasolite	**Kimzeyite (Garnet)**	**Kunzite (Spodumene)**
Katophorite (Amphibole)	**Kinoite**	**Kupletskite (Astrophyllite)**
	Koettigite	**Kyanite**

L's: Column A	L's: Column B	L's: Column C
Labradorite (Feldspar)	**Lazulite (Group)**	Limb Cast
Laguna Agate	**Lazurite (Sodalite)**	**Limestone**
Lake Superior Agate	**Lead**	**Limonite**
Lamprophyllite	Leaverite	**Linarite**
Lanthanite	**Legrandite**	**Linnaeite (Group)**
Lapis Lazuli	**Leifite**	**Lithiophilite**
Larimar Stone	**Leopard Skin Agate**	Lizardite (Kaolinite-Serpentine)
Larsenite	**Lepidocrocite**	Llanoite
Latrappite (Perovskite)	**Lepidolite (Mica)**	Lodestone
Laubmannite	**Leucite (Zeolite)**	**Lollimite**
Laueite (Paravauxite)	Leucogarnet (Garnet)	**Lollingite (Group)**
Laumontite (Zeolite)	**Leucophanite (Melilite)**	Lomonosovite
Lavender Lace Agate	**Levyne (Zeolite)**	**Lorimar**
Lavender Quartz	**Libethenite**	**Ludlamite**
Lavenite	**Libyan Desert Glass**	**Ludwigite (Group)**
	Liebigite	Lurelite
	Lignite Quartz	

≈≈≈≈≈≈≈≈≈≈≈≈≈≈≈≈≈

M's: Column A	M's: Column B	M's: Column C
Madeira Citrine	**Mesolite (Zeolite)**	**Molybdenum (Molybdite)**
Magnesioferrite (Spinel)	Metahewettite	**Monazite (Group)**
Magnesite (Calcite)	**Metatorbernite (Meta-autunite)**	**Monticellite**
Magnetite (Spinel)	**Metavariscite**	**Montmorillonite(Smectite)**
Malachite	**Meteorite (Group)**	Monzonite
Manasseite (Group)	**Mexican Lace Agate**	**Moonstone (Adularia)**
Manganaxinite (Axinite)	**Mexican Jelly Opal**	**Mordenite (Zeolite)**
Manganese	**Mica (Group)**	**Morganite (Beryl)**
Manganite	**Microcline (Feldspar)**	**Mosandrite**
Manganocalcite	**Milky Opal**	**Moss Agate (Chalcedony)**
Manjiroite (Cryptomelane)	**Milky Quartz**	**Mother of Pearl**
Marble	**Millerite**	**Mottramite (Des Cloizite)**
Marcasite (Group)	**Mimetite (Apatite)**	Moukaite
Margarite (Mica)	**Minyulite**	Mountain Leather (Actinolite)
Marialite (Scapolite)	Mirabilite	**Muggelstone**
Mariposite	**Mircoline**	Muirite
Marmatite	**Miserite**	**Mullite**
Matlockite	Mitridatite	**Muscovite (Mica)**
Melonite (Group)	**Mixite (Group)**	Myrichite
Melilite (Group)	Mochi Balls	
Meliphanite (Melilite)	Mohawkite	
Mercury	**Moldavite**	

N's: Column A	N's: Column B	N's: Column C
Nadorite	**Nephrite (Actinolite)**	**Nontronite**
Narsarsukite	**Neptunite**	**Norbergite (Humite)**
Natrojarosite (Alunite)	Niccolite	Nordenskioldine (Dolomite)
Natrolite (Zeolite)	**Nickeline (Group)**	Northupite
Natrophilite	**Nissonite**	Nosean (Sodalite)
Neotocite	**Niter**	Nullaginite (Rosasite)
Nepheline	Nitrate (Group)	Nuummit

O's: Column A	O's: Column B	O's: Column C
Obsidian	Omphacite (Pyroxene)	**Orpiment**
Ocean Spray Agate	**Onyx**	**Orthoclase (Feldspar)**
Ocho	**Opal**	Orthoferrosilite
Okenite	Opal Aura Quartz	**Osarizawaite**
Oligoclase (Feldspar)	Orbicular Agate	**Osumilite (Group)**
Olivine (Peridot)	Orbicular Jasper	Overite (Group)
		Owyheeite

≈≈≈≈≈≈≈≈≈≈≈≈≈≈≈≈≈

P's: Column A	P's: Column B	P's: Column C
Pachnolite	**Pharmocosiderite**	Pleonaste (Spinel)
Palermoite	**Phenakite**	**Plume Agate**
Palladium	Phenomenite	Polka Dot Agate
Palygorskite	Phillipsburgite	**Polybasite**
Papagoite	**Phillipsite (Zeolite)**	Polyhalite
Paracelsian (Feldspar)	**Phlogopite (Mica)**	Polyhedral Quartz
Paragonite (Mica)	Phosgenite	Polylithionite (Mica)
Paraiba Tourmaline	**Phosphophyllite**	Potch
Paravauxite (Group)	Phosphorite	Potsonte (Soapstone)
Parisite	**Picasso Stone**	Powellite
Pascoite	Pickeringite (Halotrichite)	Prase (Quartz)
Patronite	Picrolite	**Prehnite**
Paua Shell	**Picture Agate**	**Proustite**
Peacock Rock	**Picture Jasper**	Przibramite (Goethite)
Pearl	Piemontite (Epidote)	Pseudoboleite
Pecos Diamond	**Pietersite**	**Pseudobrookite**
Pectolite	**Pinakiolite (Ludwigite)**	**Psilomelane**
Pennantite (Group)	**Pink Angel Wing Dolomite**	**Pumice**
Pentlandite (Group)	**Pink Coral**	**Pumpellyite (Group)**
Periclase (Group)	Pioche	Purple Sage Agate
Pericline	**Pipestone**	**Purpurite**
Peridot	Pistacite (Epidote)	**Pyrargyrite**
Perovskite (Group)	Pitchblende	**Pyrite (Group)**
Perthite	Pitchstone	**Pyrochlore (Group)**
Petalite	Plagioclase	**Pyrolusite (Rutile)**
Petarasite (Lovozerite)	**Plancheite**	**Pyromorphite (Apatite)**
Petoskey Stone	Planerite (Turquoise)	**Pyrope (Garnet)**
Petrified Wood	Plasma Agate	**Pyrope (Rhodolite)**
Petzite	**Platinum**	**Pyrophyllite**
Phantom Calcite	**Plattnerite (Rutile)**	**Pyroxene (Group)**
Phantom Quartz		**Pyrrhotite (Quartz)**
Pharmacolite		

Q's: Column A	Q's: Column B	Q's: Column C
Quartz (Group)	Quartzite	Quenstedtite
		Quetzacoatlite

≈≈≈≈≈≈≈≈≈≈≈≈≈≈≈≈≈

R's: Column A	R's: Column B	R's: Column C
Ralstonite (Pyrochlore)	**Rhoenite**	Rose Eye Jasper
Ramsdellite	**Rhyolite**	**Rose Quartz**
Raspite	**Richterite (Amphibole)**	Roselite
Rauenthalite	Rickardite	**Rosenbuschite (Gotzenite)**
Rauvite	**Riebeckite (Amphibole)**	**Rubellite (Tourmaline)**
Realgar	**Riverstone**	Royal Plume Jasper
Reddingite	Rockbridgeite	**Ruby (Corunbum)**
Reevesite (Hydrotalcite)	**Rock Crystal Quartz**	Ruizite
Regency Rose Agate	**Romanechite**	**Rutile (Group)**
Rhodizite	**Rosasite (Group)**	**Rutillated Quartz**
Rhodochrosite (Calcite)	**Roscherite**	**Rutillated Topaz**
Rhodonite	Rose Eye Agate	**Rutillated Tourmaline**
		Ryalite

≈≈≈≈≈≈≈≈≈≈≈≈≈≈≈≈≈

S's: Column A	S's: Column B	S's: Column C
Sainfeldite	Serendibite (Aenigmatite)	**Spinel (Group)**
Salesite	**Serpentine (Group)**	**Spodumene (Pyroxene)**
Samarskite	**Shale**	Stannite (Group)
Sanbornite	**Shattuckite**	**Star Sapphire**
Sandstone	**Sheet Topaz**	**Staurolite**
Sanidine (Feldspar)	**Shell**	Steatite (Talc)
Sapphire (Corundum)	**Siderite (Calcite)**	**Stellerite (Zeolite)**
Sarabauite	**Siegenite**	**Stephanite**
Sarcolite	**Sillimanite**	Stibiconite
Sarcopside	**Silver**	**Stibiotantalite**
Sard (Carnelian)	Simpsonite	**Stibnite**
Sardonyx	**Sincosite**	**Stichtite (Hydrotalcite)**
Scapolite	**Sinhalite**	**Stilbite (Zeolite)**
Scawtite	Skarn	**Stillwellite**
Schalenblende	**Skutterudite**	Stinking Water Plume Agate
Scheelite	**Slate**	Stolzite
Scholenite (Tourmaline)	**Smithsonite**	Strawberry Quartz
Schwazite	**Smoky Citrine**	**Strengite (Variscite)**
Scholzite	**Smoky Quartz**	Stringhamite
Schorl (Tourmaline)	Snake Skin Agate	**Stromatolite**
Scolecite (Zeolite)	**Snowflake Obsidian**	Strombolite
Scorodite (Variscite)	**Soapstone (Talc)**	**Strontianite (Aragonite)**
Seamanite	**Sodalite (Group)**	**Sturmanite (Ettringite)**
Selenite	Sonolite (Humite)	**Sugilite (Osumilite)**
Selenium	Spangolite	**Sulfur**
Selestite	**Spectrolite**	**Sunstone (Apatite)**
Sellaite	**Sperrylite (Pyrite)**	Svabite
Semseyite	**Spessartine (Garnet)**	**Sylvanite**
Senarmonite	**Sphaerocobaltine (Calcite)**	**Sylvite**
Sepiolite	**Sphacerite**	**Szaibelyite**
Septarian Nodule	**Sphalerite**	
Serandite	**Sphene**	
Serape Jasper	Spider Web Jasper	
Serefina		

≈≈≈≈≈≈≈≈≈≈≈≈≈≈≈≈≈

T's: Column A	T's: Column B	T's: Column C
Taaffeite	**Thomsonite (Zeolite)**	**Tridymite**
Taikanite	Thoreaulite	**Trilobite**
Takovite (Hydrotalcite)	Thorianite	Triphylite
Talc	**Thorite**	Triploidite
Tantalite	**Thulite (Zoisite)**	Trippkeite
Tanzanite (Zoisite)	**Thunderegg**	**Trona**
Tarbuttite	Thuringite	Tsavorite (Garnet)
Tavorite (Amblygonite)	**Tiger Eye (Quartz)**	Tsilasite (Tourmaline)
Tawmawite (Epidot)	**Tiger Iron**	**Tsumebite (Brackebuschite)**
Tektite	Tigillite	Tubular Agate
Tellurite	**Tin**	**Tufa**
Tellurium	Tinstone	**Tugtupite**
Tennantite (Tetrahedrite)	Tinzenite (Axinite)	Tunnellite
Tenorite	Titanite	Tungstenite
Tennantite	Todorokite	Turgite
Tephroite (Olivine)	Topazolite (Anhydrite)	**Turquoise (Group)**
Tetrahedrite (Group)	**Topaz**	**Turritella Agate**
Thalenite	**Torbernite (Autonite)**	**Tyrolite**
Thaumasite (Ettringite)	Touchstone	**Tyuyamunite**
Thenardite	**Tourmaline (Group)**	**Tzmurdo Quartz**
	Tremolite (Amphibole)	
	Trevorite (Spinel)	

U's: Column A	U's: Column B	U's: Column C
Ulexite	**Uranocircite (Autunite)**	**Uranopilite**
Ullmannite (Cobaltite)	**Uranophane**	**Ussingite**
Unikite		**Uvarovite (Garnet)**
Uraninite		**Uvite (Tourmaline)**

V's: Column A	V's: Column B	V's: Column C
Valencianite	**Vauxite**	**Veszelyite**
Valentinite	Verdelite (Tourmaline)	**Vivianite (Group)**
Vanadinite (Apatite)	**Verdite**	Volborthite
Variscite (Group)	**Vesuvianite**	Volcanic Ash

≈≈≈≈≈≈≈≈≈≈≈≈≈≈≈≈≈≈

W's: Column A	W's: Column B	W's: Column C
Wadalite	**Wherryite**	**Wolfeite**
Wadeite	**Whewellite**	**Wolframite**
Wagnerite	**Whiteite (Group)**	**Wollastonite**
Wakefieldite	Whitlockite	Wolsendorfite
Water Opal	**Willemite**	Wonderstone Jasper
Wardite	Willemseite	Woodhouseite (Beudantite)
Wavellite	Winstanleyite	Woodwardite
Weeksite	**Witherite (Aragonite)**	**Wulfenite**
Weloganite	**Wogdinite**	Wyartite
Wermlandite	Wohlerite	

X's: Column A	X's: Column B	X's: Column C
Xanthiosite	**Xenotime**	Xitieshanite
Xanthoconite	Xiangjiangite	Xocomecatlite
		Xonotlite

Y's: Column A	Y's: Column B	Y's: Column C
Yafsoanite	Yedlinite	**Youngite**
Yagiite (Osumilite)	**Yoshimuraite**	**Yuksporite**

Z's: Column A	Z's: Column B	Z's: Column C
Zaratite	**Zinc**	**Zircon**
Zebra Agate	**Zincite**	**Zoisite (Epidote)**
Zeolite (Group)	**Zinkenite**	Zorite
Zeunerite (Autunite)	**Zinnwaldite (Mica)**	**Zunyite**

≈≈≈≈≈≈≈≈≈≈≈≈≈≈≈≈≈≈

≈≈≈≈≈≈≈≈≈≈≈≈≈≈≈≈

CHAPTER 8

BALANCING CHAKRAS VIA CRYSTAL BROADCASTING

Definition of Chakras

Although we appear to be physical, we are actually pools of energy. We live in a pulsing sea of energy that surrounds us, is inside of us, and is manifested by us. In Far Eastern philosophy, this energy is called "chi" (Taoist), "ki" (Japanese), or "prana" (Hindu). The Polynesians call this energy "mana". Regardless of the terminology, the energy is the vital force that constitutes who we are and how we feel. By paying attention to how energy enters and leaves our body and ensuring there are no blockages, we can optimize our well-being.

In both Oriental yoga and Western new age thought, chakras are energy centers which transform and distribute energy. Chakras act as inflow and outflow points for energy that enters and leaves the physical body. Chakra is the Sanskrit word for "wheel", thus named because it can be "seen" by clairvoyants as a spinning disc of energy. Chakras are not located on the physical body. Rather, they are situated on the energy body that is called the etheric body, which is approximately one inch away from the physical body. Most people, whether clairvoyant or not, can see the gray-blue band of the etheric body by focusing past someone's image and using "soft" vision. The chakras are the true healing energy centers of the body. They are the vehicles that receive and release the streams of vitality that keep our body healthy.

Chakras operate like step-down transformers for the higher energy frequencies that surround us. Without chakras, we would be bombarded by energy that would be too strong for us to withstand. Chakras process this energy and convert it into chemical, hormonal, and cellular changes in the body.

There are seven primary chakras associated with the physical body and a myriad of secondary chakra centers. The seven primary chakras include the root chakra at the base of the spine, the sexual chakra slightly below the navel, the solar plexus chakra at the midriff, the heart chakra to the right of the heart, the throat chakra at the base of the neck, the brow chakra in the middle of the forehead, and the crown chakra at the top of the head. Each chakra has a certain number of "spokes", often represented as petals of flowers in Eastern symbolism. The root chakra has the smallest number of spokes while the crown chakra has the largest. Overall well-being is contingent on the size, shape, and spin of each chakra as it enables energy to enter and leave the body as well as connecting the body with the universal life flow. Obviously, the health of the seven primary chakras is most critical to physical and spiritual well-being.

The bottom three chakras are primarily concerned with physical well-being as follows:

1. Root - will to live
2. Sexual - giving and receiving pleasure, creativity and manifestation derived from desire
3. Solar plexus - general health in body/mind/spirit, emotional balance

The top three chakras are chiefly concerned with spiritual well-being as follows:

5. Throat - communication, self-image
6. Brow - visionary abilities, connection to Universal Truth
7. Crown - pathway to the Divine, self-empowerment, spiritual center

≈≈≈≈≈≈≈≈≈≈≈≈≈≈≈≈

The middle, or fourth chakra, is the heart chakra and is considered the blending point of physical with spiritual. It connects the energy of the bottom chakras that focus on the will to live in a creative and balanced fashion with the top three chakras that focus on the attainment of Universal Truth and the path to the Divine. The heart chakra, the center of giving and receiving unconditional or Divine Love, is an assimilation point. There are also various secondary chakra points, e.g., hand, knee, that are associated with the chakra system beyond the seven primary chakras. Plus, there are higher level chakra points. This book focuses on the seven primary chakras for healing via broadcasting since these chakras are fundamental to our well-being.

Balancing Chakra Energy via Crystal Broadcasting

Sometimes the flow of energy in the chakra system becomes blocked in response to life events, particularly when basic needs are unmet. Perhaps the chakra ingress and egress point may be reduced, or the energy may flow in or out with too much force. Sometimes one chakra will over-compensate for another if there are blockages, working overtime to provide the energy that is lacking in the area with the blockage. Care must be taken not to overdevelop one chakra at the expense of the others. An open heart is nice, but if it is not balanced with other chakras, we might lack wisdom or the ability to communicate with discernment.

Some healers utilize crystals to balance the chakras when the energy goes awry. For example, a balanced root chakra provides a sense of physical well-being. However, when someone's root chakra is unbalanced, they may feel ungrounded or insecure. They may never feel safely sustained by the Earth. At its most extreme, an unbalanced root chakra can lead to conditions like anorexia where a person literally tries to starve themselves to death. Crystals can be used to bring balance to the chakra.

Typically, the crystal is placed on a weak or unbalanced chakra during the healing session. Sometimes meditations are recommended in which the person holds a specific crystal while visualizing during the meditation. Healers will recommend that a client wear the crystal that contains the healing energy, perhaps in a Native American medicine bag around their neck or in their pocket.

However, crystals can also be used to broadcast the optimal pattern for a healthy chakra. This is achieved by matching the crystal containing the balanced energy of a particular chakra center with a specific characteristic that is unbalanced in the chakra. Charts have been created for each chakra point. These charts further break out the various attributes that are associated with each chakra. For example, an open and balanced heart chakra is composed of more than one factor, e.g., joy of living, tenderness, trust in own heart, and so forth. You will need to select the crystal that matches the factor associated with your specific heart blockage. The crystal both models the balanced state plus broadcasts it 24 hours a day, 7 days a week to the universe.

The process for balancing the chakras via crystal broadcasting is outlined below:

1. Use your pendulum to determine if you are significantly out of balance in any of the seven primary chakras. Ask "Am I out of balance in any of my seven primary chakras?" If you do not wish to use a pendulum, turn to the various chakra charts and select the items that might be blocked based on your knowledge of yourself.

2. If there is an indication of a lack of balance, dowse with your pendulum to determine which of the

seven chakras require balancing. If there is more than one chakra that requires balancing, you might wish to prioritize which one to balance first rather than trying to balance all at the same time. To prioritize, you might check the percentage that each chakra is open. Remember -- if you are receiving too much energy, you may be more than 100% open which is as detrimental as being only 50% open. Once you have obtained all of the percentages, you can determine which require priority. You may want to focus on balancing the one that is, for example, only 60% open versus the one that is 88% open.

3. Once you have identified the chakra that needs balancing, go to that particular chakra chart in this book. Use your pendulum to determine which chakra trait(s) require assistance. This way you can consciously understand which assets are blocked from a behavioral or emotional perspective. For example, if your heart chakra needs balancing, you can access the heart chakra chart and proceed through the list of numbered items, asking, "Does the number one item (OR READ ITEM) require balancing?" "Does the number two item (OR READ ITEM) require balancing?" You may only need to balance one trait, or you may need to address more than one. If you are receiving too much energy in a chakra, you will need to re-interpret the trait. For example, if you are too open in the throat chakra, you may be verbose and long-winded.

4. After determining which chakra trait or traits need healing, create a Chakra Balancing Sheet for each trait. Do not place multiple traits or crystals on the same Chakra Balancing Sheet, even if the same chakra is involved. The Chakra Balancing Sheet consists of one column instead of two. You can make your own sheet or photocopy the one

≈≈≈≈≈≈≈≈≈≈≈≈≈≈≈≈

appearing in the appendix. Write your full name and birth date at the top of the sheet.

5. Write the name of the chakra you are balancing underneath your name and birth date, e.g., brow, heart, root. List the chakra trait you are balancing that has been identified on the chakra charts. You will ONLY list the positive trait you desire. There is no need to list the undesirable trait.

6. Procure the crystal that corresponds to the chakra trait requiring balancing. Sometimes more than one crystal is listed. If that is the case, use a pendulum to determine which of the crystals will be most beneficial. Please note that unless the color is specified, the color of the crystal is not important, e.g., pink versus green tourmaline.

7. Sometimes crystals are mixed with other crystals. If you are unable to find a pure specimen, use a pendulum to dowse to determine if the presence of other crystals will interfere. Most of the time the presence of other structures is ignored since the Chakra Balancing Sheet has specified what needs to be addressed. However, sometimes the presence of another structure acts counter-productively to the blockage you wish to clear. If you are unable to find a pure specimen, you may need to search for an alternative crystal. If you cannot find an appropriate alternative crystal, check the essential oils or Bach Flower remedies to determine if any of those formulations can be used. Place a clear quartz crystal next to the essential oil or Bach Flower essence to conduct the broadcasting.

8. After purchasing your crystal, you need to clear it. If you already own a crystal and have been using it for other purposes, you should also clear it. Crystals have the ability to retain energy from the environment. You need to ensure your crystal is clear. There are many ways to clear crystals. For

example, mix one tablespoon of sea salt with one cup of water and leave the crystal in that mixture for twenty-four hours. If you purchase large crystals, mix more salt water, retaining the ratio. Do not use regular table salt since sea salt holds purification properties that are not present in table salt based on the crystalline structure of the salt. Sea salt is sold in health food stores as well as many traditional supermarkets. If your crystal is in a jewelry setting, and you do not wish to place it in water, you may use pure salt. You can also place the crystal in the sun for several days.

9. After you have cleared your crystal, you might want to ask permission to use it for broadcasting. Ask to please grant you permission to use it for healing, just like the Native American's ask permission of the land for its use. This is a sign of respect and partnership, and your crystal will actually perform better for you.

10. Program the crystal by placing it in the palm of your left hand. Place your right hand, palm up, underneath your left hand. Read the list of "Desired Chakra Conditions" the crystal will be broadcasting, stating (you can paraphrase) "Please act as a model and broadcaster on my behalf for these new behaviors I am adopting, specifically (READ CONDITIONS)". Be sure to read the new conditions ALOUD.

11. Place your Chakra Balancing Sheet on top of the Universal Symbol.

12. After placing the Universal Symbol under the Chakra Balancing Sheet, put your crystal on top of the words describing the desirable chakra condition on your sheet of paper. You do not need to cover every word with the crystal.

≈≈≈≈≈≈≈≈≈≈≈≈≈≈≈≈

13. The time frame for resolution varies. Some chakra balancings are complete in two weeks. Others are still percolating after four months. Use the pendulum to dowse the required time frame when placing the crystal on the Chakra Balancing Sheet.

14. Remember, we live in a free choice/free will world, and sometimes unforeseen events occur that alter estimated time frames. Dowse at the end of the estimated time period to determine if the broadcasting process was completed according to the anticipated schedule. If not completed, leave the crystal in place.

15. When the broadcasting process is complete, it is a good idea to clear the crystal of the items it was broadcasting. Use the steps outlined in #8 to clear the crystal.

Colors and Crystals

Each of the seven primary chakras has a corresponding color as follows:

1. Root - red
2. Sexual - orange
3. Solar plexus - yellow
4. Heart - green
5. Throat - blue
6. Brow - indigo
7. Crown - violet

Often healers will use crystals to balance chakras that relate to their corresponding colors since colors carry specific vibrations. However, in crystal broadcasting there may not be a correlation between the color of the chakra and the color of the crystal. Remember, broadcasting utilizes the molecular structure of the crystal, aligning the vibration of your intention with the molecular frequency of the crystal that represents that intention. Based on the way the Universal

≈≈≈≈≈≈≈≈≈≈≈≈≈≈≈≈

Symbol translates the crystalline structure, color is not always a factor.

≈≈≈≈≈≈≈≈≈≈≈≈≈≈≈≈

The following Chakra Balancing Sheet provides an example of how to complete the sheet.

SAMPLE CHAKRA BALANCING SHEET

Name: Anne Brewer

Birth Date: December 12, 1953

CHAKRA TO BE BALANCED:

Heart

DESIRED CHAKRA CONDITION:

Capacity to give and receive unconditional love, giving and receiving love without any ties or expectations, compassion

≈≈≈≈≈≈≈≈≈≈≈≈≈≈≈≈

Crown Chakra: Connection with the Divine, Spiritual Center

Crown Chakra Conditions	Crystals
Connection with the Divine Creator, aligned with spirituality	• Amethyst • Clear Quartz • Sugilite
Can tap into internal Divine wisdom and understanding, sees Divine within, links illumined spiritual mind with universal truth	• Hematite • Purple Sage Agate • Tourmaline
Serene, harmonious, peaceful	• Almandine
Easily achieve state of meditation	• Iolite
Empowered energetically, allow Divine Light to enter	• Phenacite • Star Garnet
Strong interrelationship between high self and personality, self-realization	• Garnet • White Onyx
All parts of self well-integrated, aligned, living in purpose	• Rhodonite
Able to serve others	• Tinstone
Blockages due to constrictions or spin distortions	• Golden Topaz

≈≈≈≈≈≈≈≈≈≈≈≈≈≈≈≈

Brow Chakra: Visionary Abilities

Brow Chakra Conditions	Crystals
Third eye connection, psychic/telepathic hook-up, intuitive	• Amethyst • Angel Wing Agate
Able to see the big picture, expanded viewpoint	• Antigorite
Clear vision, perception, connection to Universal Truth	• Apache Tear • Iolite
Execution of inspirations/visions	• Tanzanite • Topaz
Have focus for life, personal priorities support ideals	• Phillipsite
Belief in limitless potential for everyone and everything	• Pyrite
Self introspection, insight	• Chrysoprase
Past life recall	• Carnelian
Knowing, aligned with personal truth	• Onyx
Blockages due to constrictions or spin distortions	• Ruby

≈≈≈≈≈≈≈≈≈≈≈≈≈≈≈≈

Throat Chakra: Communication, Self-image

Throat Chakra Conditions	Crystals
Clear communication	• Angelite
Strong self-image, ability to communicate powerfully based on self-truth	• Aegirine • Chrysocolla
Inspiration of others via communication	• Carnallite
Loving expression, speaking from the heart	• Albite
Communication of inner self, intimate expression	• Red Jasper
Communication of self through life's work, connection of mind to higher spiritual centers	• London Blue Topaz
Communication of truth, truthful expression	• Aquamarine • Purple Sage Agate
Comfortable with silence	• White Onyx
Loyal, reliable	• Malachite • Yellow Zircon
Problem solving, inductive and deductive reasoning	• Citrine
Blockages due to constrictions or spin distortions	• Black Agate

≈≈≈≈≈≈≈≈≈≈≈≈≈≈≈≈

Heart Chakra: Giving and Receiving Love, Divine Love

Heart Chakra Conditions	Crystals
Blending of physical with spiritual	• Rutilated topaz
Capacity to give and receive unconditional love, giving and receiving love without any ties or expectations, compassion	• Beryl • Moss Agate
Alignment with Divine Love	• Rose Quartz
Trust in own heart, know and trust feelings	• Kunzite
Joy of living, open to all possibilities	• Chalcedony
Positive attitude about accomplishing	• Danburite
Heartwholeness, priority of heart over brain	• Adamite • Ajoite • Obsidian
Tenderness, empathy, acceptance	• Alabaster
Living in the now	• Bloodstone
Tranquillity	• Jade
Blockages due to constrictions or spin distortions	• Phlogopit

≈≈≈≈≈≈≈≈≈≈≈≈≈≈≈≈

Solar Plexus Chakra: General Health in Body/Mind/Spirit, Emotional Balance

Solar Plexus Chakra Conditions	Crystals
General health in body/mind/spirit	• Moldavite
Emotional balance, personal power	• Dioptase • Emerald • Kunzite
Flexible, open to change	• Lepidolite • Riverstone
Right (intuitive) and left (linear) brain balance	• Tiger Eye
In flow with surroundings	• Anhydrite • Peridot
Enthusiastic, full of vitality	• Azurite • Spinel
Able to recharge and revitalize	• Diaspor
Power to enact	• Plancheite
Tolerant and accepting of self and others	• Aquamarine
Blockages due to constrictions or spin distortions	• Calcite • Moldavite

≈≈≈≈≈≈≈≈≈≈≈≈≈≈≈≈

Sexual Chakra: Giving and Receiving Sexual Pleasure, Creativity

Sexual Chakra Conditions	Crystals
Giving and receiving sexual pleasure	• Boulder Opal
Able to easily manifest	• Amber • Cat's Eye • Sapphire
Sexual energy, sensuality	• Black Opal
Deep desires	• Rhodochrosite
Invigorating of self and others	• Uranophane
Ease and openness regarding sex	• Scolecite
Creativity, inspiration	• Azurite
Blockages due to constrictions or spin distortions	• Black Tourmaline

≈≈≈≈≈≈≈≈≈≈≈≈≈≈≈≈

Root Chakra: Will to Live

Root Chakra Conditions	Crystals
Will to live, rooted in life	• Green Topaz
Life energy, vital force, survival	• Sunstone
Grounded, centered, secure	• Rhyolite
Feel comfortable with/in physical body	• Rhoenite • Selestite
Courageous, confident	• Agate • Chrysocolla
Aware of body's needs and cater to them	• Okenite
Nurture and sustain self and others lovingly	• Rhoenite
Tenacious, have stamina	• Petalite
Live in harmony with the Earth, easily experience Earth's cycles	• Boji Stones
Vitality	• Copper • Mica
Blockages due to constrictions or spin distortions	• Aquamarine • Snowflake Obsidian

≈≈≈≈≈≈≈≈≈≈≈≈≈≈≈≈

≈≈≈≈≈≈≈≈≈≈≈≈≈≈≈≈

APPENDIX

≈≈≈≈≈≈≈≈≈≈≈≈≈≈≈≈

≈≈≈≈≈≈≈≈≈≈≈≈≈≈≈≈

RESOLUTION SHEET

Name: ______________________________

Birth Date: ______________________________

New Conditions	Prior Conditions

≈≈≈≈≈≈≈≈≈≈≈≈≈≈≈≈

CHAKRA BALANCING SHEET

Name: ______________________________

Birth Date: ______________________________

CHAKRA TO BE BALANCED: ______________________________
DESIRED CHAKRA CONDITION: ______________________________ ______________________________ ______________________________ ______________________________ ______________________________ ______________________________ ______________________________ ______________________________ ______________________________

≈≈≈≈≈≈≈≈≈≈≈≈≈≈≈≈

UNIVERSAL SYMBOL

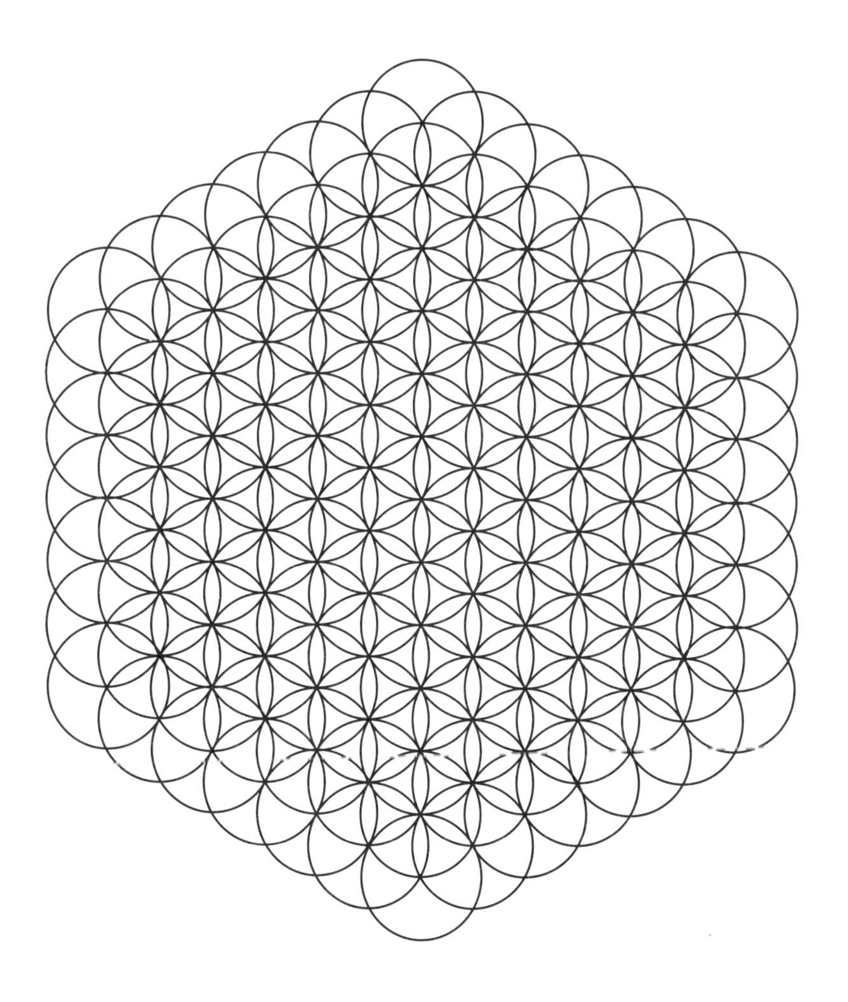

≈≈≈≈≈≈≈≈≈≈≈≈≈≈≈≈≈

≈≈≈≈≈≈≈≈≈≈≈≈≈≈≈≈

RETAIL SOURCES

Gemstones, Crystals, Minerals

Art By God
3705 Biscayne Boulevard
Miami, Fl, 33137
1-800-940-4449

Avalon Crystals
PO Box 1010
Clinton, WA, 98236
1-360-341-3427
www.neatstuff.net/avalon/

Becker's Mineral Market
PO Box 130
Penngrove, CA, 94951-0130
877-792-0700
www.beckersminerals.com
Forrest@Beckersminerals.com

Coolrox Limited
PO Box 14591
Gainesville, FL, 32604-2591
352-378-6026
www.coolrox.com
andrew@coolrox.com

Earth Minerals
PO Box 1871
Glendale, AZ, 85311
602-934-5889
www.earthminerals.com/default.asp
Chritine@Earthminerals.com

≈≈≈≈≈≈≈≈≈≈≈≈≈≈≈≈

Excelsior Gem Gallery
PO Box 232
Park Rapids, MN, 56470
218-573-3036
www.comevisit.com/excelsior
Egems@web-gems.com

Gem Resources International
PO Box 653
Long Lake, MN, 55356-0653
612-588-7373
www.gemresources.com
gri@gemresources.com

Minerals and More
PO Box 371
Bethel, OH, 45106
513-734-1359
web.gcis.net/minmor/
minmor@choice.net

Mining Center
Diagonal 380-308
Kennedy Building, Lima 18 Peru
51-14-465043
www.mineralart.com/mineperu
faro@amauta.rcp.net.pe

Pickens Minerals
610 N. Martin Avenue
Waukegan, IL, 60085-3436
847-623-2823
www.pickensminerals.com
reo@pickensminerals.com

≈≈≈≈≈≈≈≈≈≈≈≈≈≈≈≈

United Gem Dealers Syndicate, Inc.
535 N. Broadway Avenue, Suite #3
Sylacauga, AL, 35150
256-249-2700
www.ugds.com
greg@ugds.com

The Wijk bij Duurstede Rockshop
Goudse Steen 15
N1-3961 XS Wijk bij Duurstede
The Netherlands
home.wxs.nl/~dvisser/listfram.htm
dvisser@wxs.nl.

Books

Love is in the Earth, A Kaleidoscope of Crystals
by Melody
Earth-Love Publishing House - Wheat Ridge, CO

Michael's Gemstone Dictionary
Judithann H. David and JP Van Hulle
Affinity Press - Orinda, CA

Dowsing Contacts

The American Society of Dowsers
PO Box 24
Danville, Vermont, 05828
802-684 3417

≈≈≈≈≈≈≈≈≈≈≈≈≈≈≈≈

≈≈≈≈≈≈≈≈≈≈≈≈≈≈≈≈

ABOUT THE AUTHOR

Anne Brewer was born in Louisville, Kentucky. She spent seventeen years in corporate assignments, working for companies like Macy's, AT&T, and Sprint in the area of strategic marketing. During her corporate career, she held the responsibilities of National Manager for AT&T's Calling Card operations and Vice-President of Consumer Marketing for Sprint's residential long distance sales. She also wrote a textbook on marketing principles titled *The Marketer's Guide to Media Vehicles, Methods, and Options*. Anne established her own marketing consulting company in 1992, called InterLink, and began working as a consultant with Fortune 500 firms.

During her business career, Anne began reading about metaphysical principles and enrolling in classes on new age teachings. As her telepathic abilities grew, Anne utilized the writing skills she learned in the business world to record the information she was receiving from her guides and teachers. In 1998, she published her first metaphysical book, *The Power of Twelve, A New Approach to Personal Empowerment.* This book is about her personal journey toward fulfillment and self-actualization based on information received from a group of spirit guides devoted to increasing the personal power of the human race. Her second book, *Breaking Free to Health, Wealth, and Happiness, 100's of Powerful Ways to Release Limiting Beliefs*, describes many of her healing modalities. Both books have also been translated into German.

Anne conducts seminars on topics such as "Achieving 12-Strand DNA Consciousness", "Finding Your Perfect Mate", "Eliminating Obstacles to Prosperity", "Understanding Your Path and Purpose", and "Living in Euphoria". She also conducts private sessions. Her metaphysical client base extends internationally. She lives in Prairie Village, Kansas with her husband

≈≈≈≈≈≈≈≈≈≈≈≈≈≈≈≈

and perfect mate, David Beaulieu, and her son Andrew.

To contact Anne Brewer for a personal appointment, to purchase books and tapes of Anne's classes, or to schedule a workshop:

InterLink
5252 W. 67th Street
Prairie Village, KS 66208
913-722-5498 (phone)
913-722-5497 (fax)
www.annebrewer.com
info@annebrewer.com

≈≈≈≈≈≈≈≈≈≈≈≈≈≈≈≈

INTERLINK PRODUCTS	
The Power Of Twelve, A New Approach to Personal Empowerment Anne's remarkable true story of her DNA recoding is of great assistance to all of us who desire to achieve our full evolutionary potential. This transformative book includes powerful channeled instruction and holistic balancing modalities to quicken our manifestations, and clear our path to the love frequency. The first step-by-step book of it's kind, Anne outlines the empowering and approachable process of DNA recoding. We follow her exponential growth as she embraces her new capacity for high level functioning, including greatly increased psychic abilities. As she releases debilitating emotions of fear and guilt and learns to manifest her desired financial goals, her report becomes a love story where she finds and meets her perfect mate. This is a story of fulfillment of soul purpose that all of us can partake. Paperback book, 356 pages.	$17.95 plus shipping Author's Discount 20% - 40% off pending quantity
Breaking Free to Health, Wealth, and Happiness, 100's of Powerful Ways to Release Limiting Beliefs A collection of healing modalities designed to help quickly heal serious issues at the soul level so you can break free to create your dreams. Anne skillfully identifies common life issues and presents ways to repattern your responses in order to connect with the outcomes you truly want. Contains adventures in imagery, aromatherapy, creativity building, energy exchanging and clearing, and sensuality to identify limiting beliefs and transform them into positive realities. Covers the areas of well-being, relationships, purpose, wealth, spirituality, and new age insights. Paperback book, 243 pages.	$15.95 plus shipping Author's Discount 20% - 40% off pending quantity

≈≈≈≈≈≈≈≈≈≈≈≈≈≈≈≈

INTERLINK PRODUCTS (Continued)	
How to Use A Pendulum, A Simple Course in Dowsing If you wish to enhance your telepathic skills, you can begin the process by learning to dowse with a pendulum. Skilled dowsers can obtain a wide range of information, for example which vitamin and mineral supplements are necessary for good health and what is the optimal dose, the location of missing house keys, and information from spirit guides. 15 pages, spiral bound.	$12.00 plus shipping
Glass Pendulum Hand made pendulums by InterLink. These pendulums are lightweight for beginning dowsers.	$10.00 plus shipping
Brass Pendulum Hand made pendulums by Joe Smith of the Dowsing Society. Joe's pendulums are well-balanced due to a combination of his craft and the love he infuses into his pendulums.	$20.00 plus shipping
Find Your Perfect Mate Are you *still* searching for your partner? You may have barriers that inhibit your ability to meet him or her. For example, most people only resonate at 60% (or less) conviction that their true love exists. How can you expect to find your mate without total belief in their existence? Plus there are additional barriers that might be preventing you from connecting. Learn about your blockages toward finding your true love and *clear* them. Anne has based this course on her true life story in which she found her perfect mate and husband, David, in a three month time period. Human beings were not intended to live in solitary situations since we are innately communal beings. There really is another person with whom you were intended to share your life. You simply need to learn the technique for finding them. 5 hours of tapes and written materials.	$50.00 plus shipping

≈≈≈≈≈≈≈≈≈≈≈≈≈≈≈≈

INTERLINK PRODUCTS (Continued)	
Releasing Soul Barriers to Health, Wealth, and Happiness: Soul Clearing For centuries we have wondered why some people have the better things in life and others don't. According to Anne, it's our soul programs that block us from having everything we want in life. Anne teaches how to identify the source of the blockages and remove them. You can break free from limitations using simple techniques that rely on accessing the superconscious and asking it to heal you. Once you are repatterned, improved behaviors occur. Anne bases her teachings on the ancient Polynesian Huna philosophy that says the soul consists of three parts -- the subconscious, conscious, and superconscious. We may have conscious desires, but our subconscious or superconscious may not "allow" us to proceed. For example, we may want to manifest financial success but have past life vows of poverty that tell our inner soul that "money is not spiritual". Now, you can learn Anne's clearing techniques to identify and clear blocks that prevent you and others from achieving health, wealth and happiness. **Course:** Includes an explanation of the Huna philosophies and how soul clearing works, how to use a pendulum to dowse for superconscious information, introduction to your personal spiritual committee, and some beginning soul clearing techniques. Provides the charts and the research process used to determine soul blockages, gives an explanation of the most prevalent soul blockages that need clearing, and describes how to clear those blockages. Also used for depossession work, rescinding past life vows, removing curses, and property clearings. 13 hours of tape and dowsing charts and written materials.	$150.00 plus shipping

≈≈≈≈≈≈≈≈≈≈≈≈≈≈≈≈≈

INTERLINK PRODUCTS (Continued)	
Increasing Abundance Does abundance elude you? Do you utilize positive affirmations in an attempt to get what you want but encounter very little success? Do you wonder why other people have the perfect job, a great mate, a terrific family, and good health while you struggle to feel satisfied with your life? When you align your expectations to anticipate abundance and come up empty, there are usually blocks at the subconscious and superconscious levels that create barriers to plenitude, be it health, wealth, or happiness. Those blocks can come from previous lifetimes where you made soul commitments to poverty or chastity, harsh life lessons in past lives that cause you to undermine your abundance due to guilt or shame, or programs in the collective conscious that make you feel undeserving on a subconscious level. Learn what blocks exist and how to *clear* them. 4 hours of tape and written materials.	$40.00 plus shipping
Euphoria: Methods for Removing Resistance for A More Blissful Life Euphoria is a state of being when time ceases to exist, the senses absorb maximum pleasure, and elation characterizes one's outlook -- one is "high" on life. Besides feeling good, euphoria actually improves physical health and mental focus by creating coherence between the brain and the heart. Unfortunately, because we unintentionally block euphoria by creating resistance, the average person experiences very little euphoria. Anne has developed healing modalities based on knowledge of the ancient Polynesian Huna philosophy. Learn some clearing techniques for removing blockages to euphoria and align with maximum pleasure. You deserve it! 4.5 hours of tape and written materials.	$40.00 plus shipping

≈≈≈≈≈≈≈≈≈≈≈≈≈≈≈≈

INTERLINK PRODUCTS (Continued)	
Harmonious Relationships How many times did you observe the friction between your parents and say, "That won't happen to me when I get married". Yet, after finding your true love and living together awhile, disharmony started to develop. Or maybe after experiencing an unsuccessful relationship, you have decided it's not worth the effort to get involved again. Or perhaps you have never entered a relationship because you believe all relationships sour with time. Relationships can be joyful, harmonious, and uplifting as long as the energy between two people is mutually compatible. Learn about the types of energy patterns that disrupt relationships and how to clear them. Clear soul level barriers that interfere with experiencing resonance with a partner. It is much easier to maintain a positive intimate alliance when the energy supports it. This course is recommended for *both singles and couples* who desire harmonious relationships. 5 hours of tape and written materials.	$50.00 plus shipping
Crystal Broadcasting, Using Crystals to Remove Blocks and Barriers Anne has developed many repatterning methods in her healing work to change the energy blueprint and remove those unwanted yet persistent behaviors. This book describes one of her methods, using crystals to model and broadcast the desired traits. Crystals are combined with affirmations and sacred geometry to create a powerful healing process. The crystals broadcast the intended desire, just like crystals are used in radio broadcasting because of their excellent transmitting capabilities. Good habits can replace bad habits -- New Year's resolutions can become a reality! Paperback book, 148 pages.	$15.95 plus shipping Author's Discount 20% - 40% off pending quantity

* Kansas residents must add 6.851% sales tax to all items.

≈≈≈≈≈≈≈≈≈≈≈≈≈≈≈≈≈